D0483682

ACTION PLANS
80 Student-Centered Language Activities

Marion Macdonald   Sue Rogers-Gordon

NEWBURY HOUSE PUBLISHERS, INC.
ROWLEY, MASSACHUSETTS 01969
ROWLEY • LONDON • TOKYO

1984

Library of Congress Cataloging in Publication Data

Macdonald, Marion.
   Action plans.

   Bibliography: p.
   Includes index.
   1. Language and languages--Study and teaching.
I. Rogers-Gordon, Sue. II. Title.
P51.M29   1984   418'.007   83-19471
ISBN 0-88377-385-6

Cover design by Barbara Frake

NEWBURY HOUSE PUBLISHERS, INC.

Language Science
Language Teaching
Language Learning

ROWLEY, MASSACHUSETTS 01969
ROWLEY • LONDON • TOKYO

Printed in the U.S.A.

First printing: March 1984
   5   4   3

Preface

The teaching approach which led to this book is the result, in part, of our experiences at the School for International Training in Brattleboro, Vermont. In that small and close-knit community of teachers, teacher trainers, and students, we discussed, debated, and exchanged ideas about what works in the ESL and foreign language classroom and why. We were convinced, of course, that learning is most effective when it develops from the interests and motivations of the student.

This conviction led us to consider whether textbooks and teaching strategies do in fact promote student-centered learning. We found that while there are many innovative textbooks written by proponents of student-centered learning, language teachers usually do not have the time to look through them all to try to find an activity appropriate for a specific lesson. At the same time, teachers can and do develop creative ways to reach their students. They devise their own activities, activities which are often highly successful although not widely disseminated, for in the ordinary course of events teachers seldom have the opportunity to share them with colleagues.

In Brattleboro and later in our own teaching, we discovered how valuable that sharing can be, and we decided to compile a collection of student-generated activities for ESL and foreign language classes, drawing on contributions from many members of the language teaching profession. All the activities selected for inclusion reflect our belief that achieving student involvement in language learning requires a special teaching approach—one with less dependency on the textbook and more willingness to improvise and experiment with new ideas.

Action Plans is eclectic in nature and makes no attempt to be comprehensive in its coverage of grammatical structures. Intended for those teachers who have come to see the value of student-centered language learning, it offers activities in a framework which allows students to generate their own language with minimal interference from the teacher. We hope that teachers who use it will make their own modifications, add new variations, and expand the collection with ideas which have "worked" for them.

Acknowledgments

In compiling this volume, we have drawn extensively from ideas and techniques contributed by our fellow students and teachers of the Master of Arts in Teaching Program at the School for International Training of the Experiment in International Living, Brattleboro, Vermont. Additional help was provided by the teaching staff of the English and Foreign Language Programs of the Experiment. The work of Dr. Earl Stevick, Dr. Caleb Gattegno, Dr. Georgi Lozanov, and the late Charles Curran has also added valuable insights to our teaching philosophy.

We are indebted to the following creative teachers who shared some of their most effective teaching ideas with us:

From Shari Berman came permission to use Tongue Twisters (21), Slide-Tape Shows (29), Conversations of an Eraser and Pencil (64), Extemporaneous Acting (74) and with Ursula Raeth, Comparatives through Geography (4). Harlan Harris and Ursula Raeth coauthored Bingo Tic-Tac-Toe (2). Paul LeVasseur and Mark Shullenberger contributed Fiddigogo (15), Poems to Music (22), and Idioms to Music (77). Eugene Parulis proposed Guess It Right (43) and Amnesia (62). Discovering the Town (24), Neighborhoods (26), Life-Size Pictures (30), and Drawing the Students' Homes (34) were submitted by Steve Robinson.

Philip Stantial was responsible for Got a Word (11), Using Pictures as a Diagnostic Tool (40), Which Way? (41), and In What Manner? (61).

Gaylord Barr and Sue Rogers-Gordon contributed Lessons of the Week in Review (59); Sue Doyle, Personality Poster (44); Reed Goldsmith, Obstacle Course (6); and Nina McCoy, Field Trip Follow-Up (31). From Pat Moran came Chain Story (55); Robert Quinn, Verbal Volleyball (8); Janice Rogers suggested Once More with Feeling (65); and Robert Wachman described The Five-Story Building (50).

Teachers in the English Language Program of the Experiment proposed a number of their favorites: Finding Out about the Community (28), Personality Capsule (33), Picture Interview (36), Picture Narrative (42), Picture Memory Game (45), Back-to-Back Directions (47), Do as I Say (49), Cross-Cultural Skits (73), and Paired Interviews on the First Day of Class (78).

Others who shared some of their more successful classroom ideas were Sergio Duarte, who contributed three of the Foreign Language Department's most effective ideas, Creating a Small Town (46), Building a Class Dream House (54), and Spin-a-Question (75). Jean O'Loughlin was responsible for the special twist to "Dear Abby" (14); Teryl Lundquist, Request a Service

(72); Gordon Mathews, Story Sequence from Unrelated Pictures (38); and David Miller-Siegal, Tales of a Traveler (20). Deborah Wilson was the contributor of Rod Figures (52).

The Counseling-Learning Institute in East Dubuque, Ill., kindly approved our description of a General Procedure for Language Taping (56) and the Post-taping Transcript Session (57).

McGraw-Hill Book Publishers permitted us to include Evasion (9), an adaptation of Gertrude Nye Dorry's What's My Name? from *Games for Second Language Learning,* New York, McGraw-Hill, Inc., 1966.

Three activities were excerpted from Edna Gilbert's *A Way with Words,* with the permission of the publisher. These are Omit a Verb or Two (12), Add a Word or Two (13), and Magic Ball of String (18). The book was published by Educational Solutions, 80 Fifth Avenue, New York, N.Y., in 1966. Dr. John Fanselow of Columbia University was the originator of What's It For? (70).

Pro Lingua Associates in Brattleboro, Vermont, kindly granted us permission to use Category Password (3), Concentration (5), Scrambled Sentences (7), and Cocktail Party (63) from *Index Card Games for ESL,* Experiment Press/Pro Lingua Associates, Brattleboro, Vermont, 1982. Raymond C. Clark, Editor.

Raymond Clark also told us we might include An "Operation" (66) from *Language Teaching Techniques,* another publication of Pro Lingua Associates, which came out in 1980.

Professor William Slager gave permission to use a variation of teaching passive verbs in Who Done It? (79) from an excellent article entitled "Creating Contexts for Language Practice," *TESOL Quarterly,* March 1973.

Dr. Earl Stevick was the author of Activity 51, Tell and Show, described more amply in *Teaching and Learning Languages,* New York, Cambridge University Press, 1982, pp. 138–139.

Special thanks also should go to Ruthanne Brown and Patrick Moran, our chief advisers on this project, to Margery Thompson and Steve Gordon for their critical help and patient support, and to our editor, Elizabeth Lantz.

Introduction

Why do so many ESL and foreign language learners fall by the wayside before they can ask their way to the post office, follow directions, or carry on a simple social conversation with a native speaker? Both teachers and students would agree that all too often language learning is a boring, frustrating, and threatening experience. Boring because the lesson may have no relation to the students and their world. Frustrating since the students often find it difficult to live up to their own expectations of themselves and those of the teacher. Threatening since they are measuring their progress against that of their classmates. Furthermore, many schools and colleges have reinstituted the foreign language requirement, and with this prerequisite there is the inevitable fear of failure.

Many language teachers have come to believe that it is not only the particular teaching approach which turns students off language learning, but the failure of the teacher to be aware of and apply certain underlying principles which make language learning more relevant and rewarding.

Basically, these principles suggest that students perform best and retain a foreign language more successfully when they involve themselves in the lesson by choosing what to say, write, and read in a secure, supportive environment. Whether one calls this student-centered, "humanistic," or "student-invested" learning, the main idea is that the learners themselves have a stake in the lesson. They are using language naturally as they would in real situations and are encouraged to work together cooperatively. They are not just parroting the teacher's sentences or doing controlled dialogues from a textbook but are working in pairs or small groups on their own without constant supervision from the teacher.

The activities that follow are based on these principles. Teachers will recognize many as variations that have been used by creative teachers for years. Indeed, that is just what they are, a collection of activities proved in the classroom by ESL and foreign language teachers as a way to involve students in their own language learning.

Guide to the Use of the Activities

The collection is organized in a way that we hope will be most useful to the teacher. It is divided into eight general categories which promote student initiative in the four basic skills of listening, speaking, reading, and writing. The categories are games, group narratives and writing, out-of-class activities, pictures and drawings, rod activities, tape recorder/transcript, theater techniques, and miscellaneous. Also included is a grammatical index which lists the structures which these activities practice and reinforce.

The format of this book permits the teacher to select and use an activity with ease. A sample of the format follows:

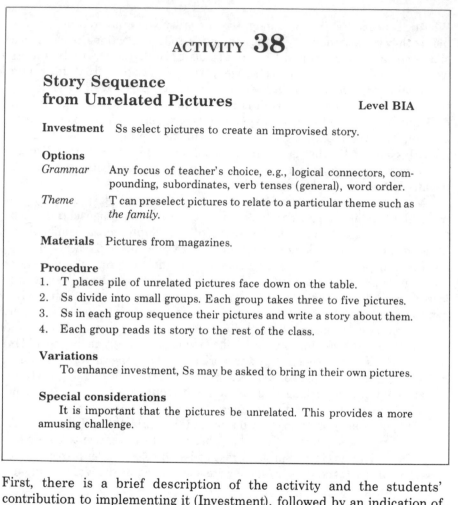

ACTIVITY **38**

Story Sequence from Unrelated Pictures

Level BIA

Investment Ss select pictures to create an improvised story.

Options

Grammar Any focus of teacher's choice, e.g., logical connectors, compounding, subordinates, verb tenses (general), word order.

Theme T can preselect pictures to relate to a particular theme such as *the family*.

Materials Pictures from magazines.

Procedure
1. T places pile of unrelated pictures face down on the table.
2. Ss divide into small groups. Each group takes three to five pictures.
3. Ss in each group sequence their pictures and write a story about them.
4. Each group reads its story to the rest of the class.

Variations
   To enhance investment, Ss may be asked to bring in their own pictures.

Special considerations
   It is important that the pictures be unrelated. This provides a more amusing challenge.

First, there is a brief description of the activity and the students' contribution to implementing it (Investment), followed by an indication of the general language level for which it is intended (Beginning, Intermediate, or Advanced). Suggested topics for grammatical, pronunciation, vocabulary, thematic, or cultural applications are provided when appropriate in the Options section. These topics may be used as the point of departure for warm-up or follow-up work for each activity. We encourage teachers to develop Options further, focusing on any aspects which they feel would be beneficial to their own students, and we hope teachers will feel free to vary and supplement the student-invested activities presented here according to the needs of their classes.

Guide to Terminology and Abbreviations

Brainstorm: A group activity in which the students spontaneously verbalize all the ideas they can think of related to a particular subject. Students should be allowed some brief time for reflection before brainstorming in a foreign language.

Feedback: At the teacher's request, students articulate their emotional and intellectual reaction to the lesson. This helps the teacher determine whether to progress, review, or modify his/her approach.

Operation: This is a teaching technique which consists of a series of events or actions which are usually universally known and logically sequenced. It is often accompanied by the manipulation of objects or gadgets. An "operation" relates to vocabulary and grammatical skills development and may involve body movement.

Transcript: A written account of sentences recorded by the students. This can be written on either the blackboard or butcher paper taped to the wall, so that students can easily read it. Using a transcript, the students can analyze, reflect on, and hopefully correct their errors themselves. The teacher can also use it as the basis for future exercises by extracting grammar, vocabulary, or pronunciation items.

Abbreviations and signs:

T = teacher	B = beginning students	BIA = all student levels
S = student	I = intermediate students	
Ss = students	A = advanced students	

Recommended Materials and Bibliography

Butcher paper: Large rolls of brown or white paper which can be used for transcripts of student-recorded sentences, class-produced maps, town plans, and murals (alternative: newsprint).

Colored felt markers: For labeling and transcript writing.

Colored construction paper: For backing pictures or creating index card games like Scrambled Sentences.

Cuisenaire rods: Small wooden blocks of ten different lengths but identical widths, each length having its own color. Valuable in getting the student to focus on using the language in such activities as constructing models of houses or towns, making geometric representations, and so forth. For those unfamiliar with Cuisenaire rods, they may be obtained through Educational Solutions, 80 Fifth Avenue, New York City, or through bookstores specializing in educational materials.

Horoscope books and magazines: For themes dealing with birthdays and personality traits.

Three-by-five index cards: For a variety of index card games, e.g., Concentration, Scrambled Sentences.

Picture magazines: For assembling a picture file that can be used in class as stimulus for creating stories and poems and making conversation.

Play money: For lessons on shopping, counting, and number practice.

Department store catalogues: For vocabulary building, shopping themes, culture exercises.

Cassette tapes: Blank tapes for group chain stories and dialogues; classical music tapes for student relaxation and listening exercises; popular music, e.g., rock, country and western, with clear lyrics which students can understand for listening comprehension.

Cassette tape recorder with microphone: For use by the students in creating and recording chain stories, dialogues, interviews, and transcripts.

Bibliography

Curran, Charles A. *Counseling-Learning in Second Languages.* Apple River: Apple River Press, 1976.

Dorry, Gertrude Nye. *Games for Second Language Learning.* New York: McGraw-Hill, Inc., 1966.

Gattegno, Caleb. *The Common Sense of Teaching Foreign Languages.* New York: Educational Solutions, Inc., 1976.

Gilbert, Edna. *A Way with Words.* New York: Educational Solutions, Inc., 1976.

Lee, W. R. *Language Teaching Games and Contests.* Oxford: Oxford University Press, 1965.

Moffett, Hames, and Betty J. Wagner. *Student Centered Language Arts and Reading, K–13.* Boston: Houghton Mifflin Company, 1976.

Stevick, Earl W. *Memory, Meaning and Method.* Rowley, Mass.: Newbury House Publishers, Inc., 1976.

Stevick, Earl W. "Teaching English as an Alien Language." In *On TESOL '76.* Eds. John F. Fanselow and Ruth H. Crymes. Washington, D.C.: TESOL, 1976, pp. 225–238.

Via, Richard A. *English in Three Acts.* Hawaii: The University Press of Hawaii, 1976.

Contents

*B = Beginning; I = Intermediate; A = Advanced

I Games

ACTIVITY 1

Actions in Sequence

Level BI

Investment   Ss brainstorm actions to be carried out in the classroom which can be made part of a gamelike activity.

Options
Grammar   Imperatives.

Materials   3×5 index cards, butcher paper.

Procedure
1. In the first class, T asks Ss to brainstorm actions that can be performed in class and be made into requests, e.g., "Go to the door," "Clean the blackboard," "Sit on the teacher's desk."
2. T writes them on butcher paper to keep for a later activity.
3. After class, T takes the transcript to arrange the list of actions into a sequence and then writes them onto separate index cards. Each card should have the previous action and the action to be performed which is underlined, e.g.,
   Card 1 Start. Go to the window.

   Card 2 After S goes to the window, close the door.

   Card 3 After S closes the door, stand on the teacher's chair.
4. In the second class, T passes out one card to each S to read silently.
5. T tells the Ss that they are to perform the activities underlined on their cards silently and in sequence. All Ss must watch closely for their turn. The S with the *Start* card begins. He is followed by the S whose card has S1's activity plus his own underlined.
6. The Ss continue performing their activities silently in sequence, and as quickly as possible until everyone has had a chance.

Special considerations
   This activity will take more than one class period in order to give the T time to write up the Ss' list of actions onto index cards.
   Index cards should *not* be numbered, to make the game more challenging.
   If the Ss have trouble understanding the exercise, they should first read the cards aloud in sequence.

ACTIVITY **2**

Bingo Tic-Tac-Toe

Investment   Ss in teams compete in making up sentences incorporating different words from the grid.

Options
Grammar   Any focus of teacher's choice, e.g., word order.

Materials   A large grid divided into 32 squares, 8 across and 4 down, prepared prior to class. Each square contains a word or a brief phrase. Strips of paper for Ss to write sentences on.

Procedure
1.   T puts up previously prepared grid with words that need review or which trigger a certain kind of sentence, e.g., usually, could, pick up, while, where, interesting.
2.   T then divides the class into several teams and assigns a number to each. The teams are given a supply of paper strips for writing sentences.
3.   T explains that the teams are to write one sentence at a time using one word from anywhere on the grid. They must write their sentences on a paper strip as quickly as possible and give them to the T.
4.   The T writes the number of the team with the first correct sentence in the appropriate square on the grid. Other teams may not use the word in that square.
5.   The team whose number appears most often on the grid is the winner.

Variations
Ss can make up the word composition of the grid.
More advanced Ss can be asked to try to use several grid words in a sentence, thereby winning more points.

Special considerations
Ss must have their sentences grammatically correct before going on to another one.

ACTIVITY 3

Category Password Level BIA

Investment   Ss think of items to fit into categories as well as adjectives to describe them for a competitive game.

Options
Vocabulary   Reinforcement of words Ss have already studied.

Materials   3×5 index cards.

Procedure
1. T gives examples of categories, e.g., kinds of public buildings, pieces of furniture. Ss then brainstorm additional categories.
2. T breaks the class into two teams (A and B) and assigns five categories to each.
3. T instructs the groups to write their category headings on the top of separate index cards. Under the headings they are to list four items that belong to the category, e.g., *category fruit*, items: apple, mango, orange, tomato.
4. S on team A draws a card from team B, then tells team A the category. S describes the first item listed in the category as well as possible without using the word itself or a synonym.
    For example, to describe an apple S may say "red, juicy, eat." Team A must guess the item by name.
5. The same S progresses as quickly as possible to the next three items on the card for the team to guess.
6. T keeps score by timing the minutes it takes each team to guess all four items in a category.
7. Team B follows the same procedure as team A. Teams keep alternating turns.

ACTIVITY 4

Comparatives through Geography   Level BIA

Investment   Ss ask and answer geographical questions using comparatives and maps in a competitive activity.

Options
Grammar   Comparatives, WH and yes/no questions.
Vocabulary   Geographical terms.
Theme   Geography.

Materials   World map.

Procedure
1. T asks for two S volunteers who have a good knowledge of geography to ask the class questions about the world map.
2. Ss divide into two teams.
3. The S volunteers take turns asking the teams questions about the map, e.g., "What is the longest river in the world . . . the highest mountain?"
4. The team which answers correctly first gets the point.

Special considerations
   Ss should have already studied comparatives.
   For beginners, it may be necessary for the S volunteers to plan and write out the questions first.
   Ss need to have a good knowledge of world geography; if not, this lesson could be based on a map of their own country.

ACTIVITY 5

Concentration Level BIA

Investment   Index cards contain words Ss need to reinforce. The gamelike nature of the activity prompts investment.

Options
Vocabulary   May have a special focus, e.g., the home, food, landscape.

Materials   Set of at least twenty 3×5 cards. Each card has a large, clearly written number on one side and a printed word or phrase on the opposite side.

Procedure
1. Ss gather in a circle seated around a table or on the floor.
2. T places the cards in the center of the circle numbered side up, randomly arranged.
3. A S chooses a number and another S or the T turns that over.
4. The first S picks another number, hoping to match the first word.
5. If the words don't match, both cards are turned to their original face-down positions.
6. The next S follows the same procedure, trying to remember the previous Ss' choices. If a match is made, S removes the two cards from the game and continues to choose pairs until he/she fails to make a match. Another S then has a turn.
7. The game continues in this manner with Ss taking turns until all the words have been matched.

Variations
   After the S makes a match, he/she will have to put the word into a sentence at that time.

ACTIVITY 6

Obstacle Course

Investment   Ss direct one another blindfolded through an obstacle course which they have set up.

Options
Grammar   Imperatives.
Vocabulary   Direction words (e.g., turn, stop, go).
Theme   Direction giving.

Materials   A blindfold, class furniture.

Procedure
1. While a student volunteer is sent out of the classroom, the rest of the class creates an obstacle course, which the volunteer must negotiate blindfolded when he returns.
2. Another S gives the volunteer precise directions for maneuvering through the obstacle course so S won't bump into anything.
3. The same procedure continues with the other Ss. Each time the obstacle course should be altered.

Special considerations
The necessary vocabulary for this exercise should already have been taught. These words include such direction-giving words as: left, right, forward, sideways, step, and turn around.

ACTIVITY 7

Scrambled Sentences Level BIA

Investment   Ss in teams unscramble sentences which they or the T may have written. The gamelike nature of this activity prompts investment.

Options
Grammar   Word order, making questions, any focus of teacher's choice.

Materials   3×5 index cards cut in half, assorted color felt markers.

Procedure
1. Before class T writes out sentences that concentrate on grammatical points or constructions which Ss have recently studied. (May use Ss' transcripts for reference.) T writes the sentences onto the cards, one word per card. All the words from one sentence should be written in the same color marker to distinguish it from the other sentences. T then scrambles the word order of each sentence.
2. T has Ss divide into groups and gives one scrambled sentence to each.
3. Ss unscramble the sentences as quickly as possible. T may award points to the fastest group, if desired.
4. Groups then rescramble the sentences, and exchange with each other.

Variations
   Ss write the sentences into their notebooks after they have unscrambled them.

   Ss make questions out of the scrambled sentences.

   Ss can do all the work from writing the sentences to putting them onto the cards.

ACTIVITY 8

Verbal Volleyball

Level BIA

Investment   Ss make up questions and answers while throwing a ball.

Options

Grammar   Verb tenses (general), subject/verb agreement, WH, yes/no, and tag questions.

Theme   Questions and answers pertaining to a specific theme, e.g., Ss' weekend activities.

Materials   A large rubber ball, sponge ball, or beanbag.

Procedure
1. T throws the ball to a particular S, and asks a question while throwing the ball.
2. While catching the ball, S must give the answer.
3. The catcher then throws the ball with a new question to another S, who catches while giving an answer.
4. Ss continue throwing and catching the ball with questions and answers.

Variations

   T can focus on subject/verb agreement. Ss choose a verb. When Ss throw the ball, they say a proper noun or a pronoun. As the other Ss catch the ball, they must give the correct subject/verb agreement; e.g., S1 says "he," and the S2 would say "runs."

ACTIVITY 9

Evasion

Investment   Ss try to trick one another into answering *yes* or *no* in a cocktail party atmosphere.

Options

Grammar   Yes/no questions.

Vocabulary   Alternative expressions for *yes* and *no,* and words to avoid commitment, e.g., maybe, perhaps, possibly.

Culture   Advanced Ss could discuss manner in which different cultures avoid giving direct answers.

Materials   Straight pins with colored heads.   *beans*

Procedure

1.   T distributes five straight pins to each S to be pinned to their collars.
2.   T tells Ss to mingle and converse with each other for about 20 minutes, as if they were at a party. They should try to trap one another into answering *yes* or *no* when asked questions during their conversations.
3.   If any S answers *yes* or *no* to a question, this S must award a pin to the person who asked the question.   *bean*
4.   When the time is up, the S with the most pins wins the game.

   beans

Variations

   T can create a real party atmosphere by bringing in refreshments.

   A setting other than a cocktail party may be used, e.g., boy meets girl or a political convention.

Special considerations

   The T tells the Ss to intersperse their questions during the conversations with other types of comments and statements, instead of solely firing questions.

II Group Narratives and Writing

ACTIVITY 10

Labeling Articles in the Classroom   Level B

Investment   Ss choose the articles in the classroom they want to label.

Options
Grammar   WH and yes/no questions.

Materials   3×5 index cards, felt markers, tape, dictionaries.

Procedure
1.   T asks Ss in turn to point out items in the classroom which they want to identify.
2.   Other Ss state the name of the item if they know it. The T supplies any words the Ss cannot come up with themselves, or the Ss can look it up in a bilingual dictionary. The T writes the words on the blackboard.
3.   Ss make labels for all the items on the blackboard, and attach them to the appropriate objects.
4.   Ss copy all the words into their notebooks.

Variations
Ss ask and answer each others' questions about items in the classroom, e.g., "What is that?" "That's a blackboard."

T can remove labels and Ss can ask the same questions of each other.

ACTIVITY 11

Got a Word?   Level BI

Investment   Ss write group stories including words they have preselected.

Options
Grammar   Any grammar focus of teacher's choice, e.g., word order.

Theme   Ss or T could decide on a theme, e.g., adventure or mystery story.

Materials   Ss' own writing materials.

Procedure
1. T asks Ss for a proper noun, a verb, a modal, an adjective, another noun, etc. (about 10 to 15 words.) T writes these words on the board. If students aren't familiar with the parts of speech, T can simplify it by asking for someone's name, something you can do, a word that tells what something looks like, etc.
2. T then has the Ss break into small groups. Each group is to write one short story which includes all the words that have been written on the blackboard. T should stress that all the members of a group should contribute to its story.
3. A representative from each group reads its story to the rest of the class.

Variations
Ss exchange stories and correct them.
T can type up corrected copies and put them into book form for all the Ss to read.

ACTIVITY 12

Omit a Verb or Two   Level BI

Investment   Ss in groups write original paragraphs as basis for a verb-omitting exercise.

Options
Grammar   Parts of speech recognition, verb tenses (general).
Theme   Ss may decide on a theme before beginning the activity.

Materials   Ss' own writing materials, dittos for T.

Procedure
1. In the first class the T has the class divide into small groups to write composite paragraphs on a topic of their choice. Each S in a group must contribute a sentence to the group's paragraph.
2. After the paragraphs are completed, Ss look them over and revise if necessary. T may help if needed.
3. T collects the paragraphs and types them onto dittos, leaving out some of the verbs following the first two sentences. (If the T wishes, other parts of speech may be omitted instead.)
4. In the second class meeting, the T distributes the dittoed paragraphs to the Ss, making sure that each S gets a paragraph from another group. Ss individually work on filling in the blanks with verbs, trying to get the tense and meaning in their proper context.
5. Ss can read their completed paragraphs aloud to the class, or T can post the paragraphs on the bulletin board, so the Ss can see the variety of possibilities in verb substitution.

Variations
Ss may write individual paragraphs.
This exercise may be used for a quiz or test the Ss write themselves.
The T may use the paragraphs for a "cloze exercise," where every fifth word is omitted.

Special considerations
This activity will take more than one class period to complete.

ACTIVITY 13

Add a Word or Two
Level IA

Investment   Each S creates a three-word sentence to which other Ss write additions until the additions no longer make a complete thought.

Options
Grammar   Logical connectors, compounding, relative pronouns, word order.

Materials   Ss' own writing materials.

Procedure
1. Ss divide into groups of 8 to 10 or remain in one group if the class is small.
2. Each S in the group writes a three-word sentence and passes it to his/her neighbor, who adds one or two words, provided the additions make a complete thought. Ss continue passing on the same sentence until they have exhausted its possibilities.
3. When Ss have finished writing sentences, T asks Ss to read their original three-word sentence and the final product.

Variation: "Chain Story"
   One S can write a sentence to begin a story. Other Ss continue adding to the story a sentence at a time.

ACTIVITY 14

"Dear Abby"   Level IA

Investment Ss in groups or individually compose letters of advice to "Dear Abby" writers.

Options
Grammar Conditionals, modals, WH and yes/no questions.

Theme Asking for advice.

Culture Ss compare social problems in U.S. and foreign cultures.

Materials Assortment of "Dear Abby" or "Ann Landers" letters clipped from newspapers.

Procedure
1. Class divides into pairs or small groups. T gives each group a "Dear Abby" letter to read and discuss among themselves.
2. T circulates among the groups to help with unfamiliar vocabulary.
3. Each group decides on the advice it wants to give the letter writer and makes up a reply. T helps if needed.
4. When groups have finished their answers, they can read their "Dear Abby" letters as well as their replies to the class.
5. T posts letters on the bulletin board so all the Ss can read them.

Variations
Ss write the original "Dear Abby" letters themselves and exchange with classmates to answer.

Lesson can be used as a basis for a cultural discussion about social problems and how they are handled in various societies.

ACTIVITY 15

Fiddigogo*

Investment   Ss use words from their own language in combination with the target language to write a paragraph, poem, or very short story.

Options
Grammar   Any focus of teacher's choice.

Culture   Ss share words from their own languages.

Materials   Ss own writing materials.

Procedure
1.   S1 thinks of a particularly expressive word in S's own language and tells it to the class.
2.   Other Ss try to guess the meaning based on its sound.
3.   Then S1 puts the word in context in an English sentence, e.g., "There was much 'fiddigogo' at the baggage claim in the airport." S1 can give additional sentences if the Ss are still having trouble guessing the meaning of the word.
4.   When Ss have guessed or have been told the meaning of the word, S1 writes it on the blackboard with the translation.
5.   The other Ss in turn propose their words following the same procedure as S1.
6.   After all the Ss have presented their words, they write short stories, poems, or paragraphs in the target language, incorporating all the words on the blackboard in their original tongue.
7.   Ss share what they have written.

Variations
   Ss can divide into groups to write composite stories.

Special considerations
   This activity is appropriate only for a multilingual class.

---

*Fiddigogo means confusion in Trukese.

ACTIVITY 16

Horoscope Watching

Level IA

Investment Ss in groups discuss, list, and compare their personality traits with the traits stated in their horoscopes.

Options
Grammar Modals, adjectives, WH and yes/no questions, verb tenses.
Theme Personality traits.

Materials Posters, magic markers, horoscope book or magazines.

Procedure
1. Prior to class T will need to prepare 12 separate lists indicating the personality traits for each horoscope sign. T lists the 12 horoscope signs and their dates on the blackboard. If some students aren't familiar with horoscope signs, the T will need to explain them.
2. The T asks the Ss the months and dates of their birth, and enters their names under the correct horoscope sign listed on the blackboard.
3. The T then asks the Ss to break up into groups according to their sign.
4. The T gives each group a list of personality traits for its own sign.
5. Each group discusses and writes these traits on a poster.
6. A group presents itself to the class. The rest of the class then states what traits they think the presenting group members have in common.
7. The presenting group then shows its poster and describes the personality traits of its sign to the class.
8. The class asks questions and discusses with the presenting group whether they agree with the horoscope.
9. Other groups take turns presenting their horoscopes. A class discussion can follow regarding astrology, its accuracy and relevance to Ss lives, etc.

Variations
Ss compare negative and positive aspects of their sign.
Ss pick out ideal mate according to the horoscope.
Ss check out previous day's horoscope in the newspaper and compare it with what actually happened (good exercise for the past tense).
Ss compare their traits with those of famous people of their sign.

Special considerations
If there are individual Ss who are the only ones with a particular sign, let them participate with another group.

ACTIVITY 17

If . . .?

Level IA

Investment   Ss make up sentences about one another using "if" clauses.

Options
Grammar   (Real or unreal) conditionals.
Theme   Professions, weekend plans, etc.

Materials   Strips of paper for writing sentences.

Procedure
1. Ss divide into two groups.
2. T directs group A to compose only the first half of "if" clause sentences, using the names of the Ss in the class, e.g., "If Isabel would get up on time. . ."
3. T then instructs group B to write only the second half of "if" clause sentences, also using the Ss' names, e.g., "Tom would be sick." Each group should work independently.
4. T puts group A's and group B's sentence halves in separate piles. Ss, taking turns, select a sentence half from each pile and read the resulting sentence aloud. The sentences may not make much sense but should prove amusing.

Variations
   Ss write complete sentences on paper strips, which are cut in half and reassembled by other Ss.
   This exercise can also be done with the unreal conditional. In such a case the Ss writing the first sentence half would use proper names, and those writing the second halves would use he/she pronouns.

Special considerations
   This should be used as a brief follow-up exercise after the T has already introduced the real and unreal conditionals.

ACTIVITY 18

Magic Ball of String
Level IA

Investment Each S contributes to a chain story using a ball of string.

Options

Grammar Any grammar focus of teacher's choice, e.g., logical connectors, modals.

Theme Ss may decide on theme before beginning the activity.

Materials A large ball of string with knots tied at various intervals (2 to 5 feet apart) or a ball of yarn of different lengths and colors knotted together.

Procedure
1. Ss form a circle, and T puts a large ball of string in the middle. The ball should have as many knots as there are Ss.
2. The first S takes the loose end of the string and begins a story. Rewinding the string into a ball, S1 continues the story until coming to a knot, at which point S1 must stop, even if in the middle of a sentence.
3. The next S takes the rewound ball and continues the story until he/she also comes to a knot.
4. The same procedure continues until all the Ss have contributed and the last of the string is unwound.

Variations
For intermediate or advanced Ss, the T may use a ball of different colors of yarn knotted together, each signifying different moods in the story, e.g., green is adventurous, blue is sad, yellow expresses gaiety. Ss should change their story to fit these moods.

ACTIVITY 19

Song Writing

Investment   Ss in groups rewrite some of the lyrics to a song in the target language.

Options
Pronunciation   Syllabification; stress intonation.

Theme   Could have special focus, e.g., love songs.

Materials   A tape or record of a song with easily understood lyrics, tape recorder or phonograph, dittos.

Procedure
1. Before class T selects a tape or record of a song in the target language and dittoes the lyrics for the class. T then underlines the words Ss will change.
2. T passes out the dittoed lyrics to the Ss, and asks them to listen to the song on the tape recorder as they follow along reading the lyrics.
3. T plays the song through again, this time asking the Ss to sing along.
4. Ss break up into small groups and "rewrite" the lyrics by changing the underlined words, making sure that the syllables of the new words match or fit into the rhythm of the song. This may have a particular focus; e.g., verbs can be replaced with synonyms or antonyms, adjectives or adverbs may be changed.
5. Groups practice their "rewritten" song among themselves.
6. Groups read or sing their new version to the class.

Variations
T puts the new version of the songs on the bulletin board for all the Ss to read.

Ss can sing each other's songs.

To make this lesson more amusing, Ss can replace key words with absurd or ridiculous substitutions, e.g., "I'm in the Mood for Love" becomes "I'm in the Mood for Lasagna."

T may stress a particular grammatical focus by underlining just verbs, adverbs, adjectives, etc.

ACTIVITY 20

Tales of a Traveler

Level IA

Investment   Ss create their own chain story about an imaginary trip the class has taken.

Options

Grammar   Adverbs of time and frequency, present perfect tense, past tense, verb tenses (general).

Theme   Taking a trip.

Materials   World map, tape recorder with microphone (optional).

Procedure
1.   T has Ss brainstorm all the adverbs of time and frequency they can think of, e.g., still, just, already, yet. T writes these on the blackboard.
2.   T then tells the class to look at the world map and select a country where they would like to take an imaginary trip.
3.   T tells the Ss to make up a chain story about this trip, concentrating on using the present perfect tense. Each S must contribute a sentence which must include one of the adverbs of time and frequency listed on the blackboard.
4.   This procedure continues until all the Ss have spoken a sentence. An example might be: "We are traveling between Mexico City and Acapulco and up to now have only gone 15 miles. We have already had two flat tires."

Variations
   This exercise can be done with the Ss saying their sentences into the tape recorder. The transcript can then be written up by the T so that the Ss may look it over and revise it, if necessary (see activity 57).

   T can have the Ss practice the sentences using one of the exercises mentioned in the Transcript Follow-up Exercises (see activity 58).

   T can propose a similar exercise using other verb tenses.

ACTIVITY 21

Tongue Twisters

Investment Ss create tongue twisters based on difficult sounds in the target language that they decide to work on.

Options
Pronunciation Sounds Ss need to work on.

Materials Dictionaries for Ss.

Procedure
1. T has Ss break up into groups.
2. Each group selects a sound they have trouble with and makes up a tongue twister for it with the help of a dictionary, e.g., "Your youthful yellow yak yawns in Yugoslavia." T moves among groups to help if needed.
3. Each group in unison presents its tongue twister to the rest of the class.
4. Ss can exchange and try to say each others' tongue twisters as quickly and accurately as possible.

ACTIVITY 22

Poems to Music   Level A

Investment   Ss contribute to writing one another's poems—inspired by music.

Options
Grammar   Any grammar focus of teacher's choice, e.g., adjectives, adverbs.

Theme   Ss may decide on a theme before beginning the activity.

Culture   Music may trigger different images to Ss from various cultures, which could lead to interesting discussions.

Materials   Classical music, e.g., "Jesu Joy of Man's Desiring," Beethoven's Pastoral Symphony, tape recorder or record player.

Procedure
1. Ss break up into groups of about five and arrange themselves in a circle around a table or on the floor. T plays classical music.
2. Ss are given 10 minutes to listen to the music and reflect on its mood before beginning to write their poems.
3. Still listening to the music, each S begins a poem on a piece of paper, writing only one line. All Ss then place their papers in the middle of their circle, and randomly choose another S's paper, and write a second line that follows the first line and the mood of the music.
4. Ss continue adding a line at a time to each other's poems. At the end of the exercise, there should be five poems done by each group. (This whole procedure of poem writing should take about 20 minutes.)
5. Ss discuss and share poems with their own group and with the other groups.

Variations
   Ss can write individual poems that the music suggests to them.
   Poems can be written up and posted on the bulletin board for other Ss to read.

III   Out-of-Class Activities

ACTIVITY 23

Scavenger Hunt

Investment   Ss plan where and how to find the items on a scavenger hunt list.

Options
Grammar   WH and yes/no questions, quantifiers.

Materials   Lists of objects to be found in the community, e.g., a map of the town from the Chamber of Commerce, a blank bill from a restaurant, a store catalogue.

Procedure
1.   T asks Ss to break up into pairs for the scavenger hunt.
2.   T gives each pair a different list of about 5 to 10 items to find and bring back to class. T should set a time limit of not more than two hours. First pair of Ss returning with all the items on their list wins a prize.
3.   Ss "show and tell" about items they have brought back.

Variations
More advanced Ss could make up the lists for each other.

Special considerations
In making up the list, T should pick only items which are free and which Ss need to ask for to obtain.

ACTIVITY 24

Discovering the Town
Level BIA

Investment Ss make a map of the town they're living in, showing the location of public buildings, stores, parks, etc.

Options

Grammar WH and yes/no questions, modals, imperatives, *there is/there are.*

Vocabulary Different types of shops, public buildings, etc.

Theme The town or neighborhood.

Materials Dittoed copies of a map of the town, large sheet of butcher paper.

Procedure
1. Before class the T draws on ditto paper a map showing the streets of the town. Only a few of the major streets are labeled. In the corner of the map is a numbered key of the buildings the Ss are to try to locate, e.g., 1. Post Office, 2. Marion's Gourmet Kitchen, 3. Gaylord's Body Shop.
2. In class the T tells the Ss they are to go into the community and ask directions to help them locate the buildings listed in the key. Ss fill in their maps to show the location of the buildings and write in the names of the unlabeled streets.
3. Ss break up into small groups or pairs and go out into the community to locate the buildings and fill in the map.
4. Back in class the Ss then make up their own large-scale town map, filling in all the missing street names as well as the names of the buildings they located. They use their own maps for reference.

Variations

The large map can be used as a basis for a direction-giving exercise. See activity 41.

Special considerations

Foreign language classes can do this activity in a local ethnic neighborhood.

ACTIVITY 25

Interviewing
Target Language Speakers
Level BIA

Investment Ss decide on people to interview, interview topics, and the procedure to follow.

Options
Grammar WH and yes/no questions, verb tenses (general), modals, reported speech.

Theme Interview subject may be a topic of Ss' choice, e.g., nuclear energy.

Culture Post-interview class discussions could focus on whether the opinions of those interviewed are culturally influenced.

Procedure
1. Ss in pairs decide which target language speaker to interview.
2. Each pair composes possible questions for interviews on a topic they have selected as a class.
3. Ss practice their questions for the interview with each other or the T.
4. Ss then set up and conduct interviews with persons they have selected. Ss should plan whether to take notes on their interview or use a tape recorder.
5. Back in class, Ss give brief reports on their interviews. If the class focused on a special topic or theme, Ss can compare differing points of view of the people interviewed.

Variations
Beginning Ss in pairs conduct a series of interviews with the same individual over a period of time. The first interview can be limited to very simple information gathering, subsequent ones become progressively more difficult in content.

Special considerations
For younger students T may need to suggest how to set up interviews, whom to contact, etc.

ACTIVITY **26**

Neighborhoods

Investment   Ss compose questions to ask inhabitants of different ethnic and/or socioeconomic neighborhoods.

Options

Grammar	WH and yes/no questions, prepositions, modals, *there is/there are*, and verb tenses (general).
Vocabulary	Words pertaining to direction giving.
Theme	Any focus, e.g., community and the family.
Culture	In a large city the Ss could explore different ethnic neighborhoods and compare impressions.

Materials   Two large-scale maps of the town or city where the Ss are studying, Ss' own writing materials.

Procedure

1.   Before class the T outlines with a felt marker the various ethnic and/or socioeconomic neighborhoods of the city on two identical maps. One map is hung in front of the class. The other is cut up according to the neighborhood boundaries, with a description of each written on the back, e.g., Chinese, working-class neighborhood.

2.   T tells the Ss that they are going to conduct interviews with people who live in the neighborhoods indicated on the map in front of the room.

3.   The class then discusses the types of questions they want to ask in their interviews. T writes their suggestions on the board.

4.   The class divides into pairs or small groups. The T gives each group a map section of the neighborhood they would like to investigate.

5.   The S groups then look over the suggestions on the board, and plan the questions they will ask in their neighborhood.

6.   T tells Ss they must find their way to the neighborhoods by referring to their maps and asking people directions.

7.   The groups then go out and conduct the interviews in their assigned neighborhoods. They must interview at least three people.

8.   Each group reports back to the class on the questions they asked and their findings.

9.   The Ss then discuss and compare their neighborhoods.

Variations

The Ss' interview questions may have a specific focus, e.g., What are the problems in each neighborhood?

If Ss are familiar with the city, they may divide the map up into neighborhoods and choose which ones they want to visit.

To extend the activity, the T can arrange to meet the Ss for lunch at a restaurant after their interviews. The Ss will have to ask people on the street directions on how to get there.

Special considerations

For high school students parental consent may be necessary to send Ss into the neighborhoods.

ACTIVITY 27

Preparing and Cooking Food
for a Class Party
Level BIA

Investment Ss plan their own class party and prepare the dishes.

Options
Grammar Count and noncount nouns, imperatives, WH and yes/no questions.

Vocabulary Food and recipes, ingredients, measurements.

Theme Cooking, foods, and recipes.

Culture Ss compare food and menus of the target language culture and their own.

Materials Ingredients for recipes, cooking utensils, cookbooks.

Procedure
1. Ss discuss a possible menu for their class party. T writes their suggestions on the blackboard.
2. Ss decide on a menu.
3. Small groups or pairs of Ss choose a dish they want to prepare, and then find a recipe for it in the cookbooks the T has provided.
4. Ss copy their recipes and decide on the amount of ingredients needed to prepare the dish for the whole class.
5. The Ss list all the ingredients they need for a general shopping list.
6. Volunteer Ss shop for the food.
7. At the party, Ss divide into their groups to prepare the dish they have chosen. One S in a group reads out the directions, while the others prepare. Then on with the party!

Variations
   After the party Ss can exchange recipes and explain how they made them.
   A S can teach the others how to make one of his/her national dishes.

Special considerations
   T needs a place for Ss to prepare and cook the food and have the party.
   Before this activity, T should have taught measurements.

ACTIVITY **28**

Finding Out about the Community Level IA

Investment   Ss choose and visit appropriate places to find out information about the community.

Options

Grammar	Reported speech, *there is/there are*, asking questions.
Theme	Finding information.
Culture	As a result of this activity, Ss may discover the community's sociological makeup, its traditions and customs.

Materials   Blackboard.

Procedure
1. Ss brainstorm types of information they want to find out about the host community, e.g., movie theater schedules, social activities, types of restaurants, concert series, educational opportunities. T writes these on the blackboard.
2. T asks Ss where they can go to find these things out. If they don't know, T gives suggestions, e.g., chamber of commerce, bookstores, and lists these on the blackboard.
3. Ss in pairs or small groups pick separate areas of interest to investigate.
4. Ss go out into the community to get their information. They should bring back pamphlets, schedules, etc., and take notes so that they will be prepared to discuss their findings with the class.
5. Each group reports to the class. The information can then be posted for Ss to look at.

Variations
   Ss in pairs can be dropped off in different surrounding communities to try to find out as much as possible about the town by talking to local citizens in public offices, restaurants, or shops.

Special considerations
   Transportation will need to be provided.
   Foreign language classes can do this activity in a local ethnic neighborhood.

ACTIVITY **29**

Slide-Tape Shows
Level IA

Investment Ss create a slide-show coordinated with a narrative and/or dialogue they have written.

Options

Grammar   Any focus of teacher's choice, e.g., modal perfects, subordinators and logical connectors, conditionals, two-word verbs, *there is/there are*.

Theme   Any focus.

Culture   Could focus on an activity typical of the target language culture or the Ss' own.

Materials Camera, film, tape recorders, slide projector.

Procedure
1. T asks Ss to break up into groups of four to five to discuss and plan a slide-sound show based on a short story or an "operation"* they create.
2. Groups first sketch their plot outline and plan the pictures they want to take to coordinate with it.
3. Each group plans where and when to take its pictures.
4. The groups then go out to the community to take the pictures. Ss then have their pictures developed.
5. After the pictures have been developed, the groups sequence them. They can write a narrative and/or dialogue to coordinate with their pictures. T can help if necessary.
6. When the Ss are satisfied with the quality of their narratives, they tape them.
7. One or two groups a week are given the opportunity to practice the coordination of their tapes with the slide projector. These groups practice while other groups are working on another project.
8. After the groups have each had the chance to practice and perfect their slide-tape shows, they present them to the class.

Special considerations
This project may be done over a period of a few weeks or a semester.

---

*See activity 66.

IV   Pictures and Drawings

ACTIVITY **30**

Life-Size Pictures Level B (Children)

Investment   Ss draw and describe life-size pictures portraying themselves in future professions.

Options
Grammar   Imperatives, verb + infinitive, WH and yes/no questions, present perfect tense.

Vocabulary   Words pertaining to professions.

Theme   Professions.

Materials   Butcher paper, felt markers or crayons.

Procedure
1. T has Ss discuss what professions they would like to have when they are adults.
2. T then gives each S a sheet of butcher paper long enough to trace their body outlines.
3. Ss break into pairs. While S1 in each pair lies on the piece of paper, S2 traces his/her body outline. Ss reverse.
4. Ss then color and fill in their own outlines, according to what they think they would like to be as adults, e.g., firefighter, doctor, rock star.
5. Ss then tell the class about their pictures, and answer questions about them.

ACTIVITY 31

Field Trip Follow-up

Level B (Children)

Investment   Ss use previous day's field trip as basis for a written exercise.

Options

Grammar   Past tense, WH and yes/no questions, adjectives, adverbs, *there is/there are.*

Vocabulary   Words pertaining to the countryside.

Theme   A picnic, sightseeing trip, a visit to the countryside.

Materials   Butcher paper, different-colored felt markers or crayons.

Procedures
1. Following a field trip, T tells Ss they are going to draw a group mural on butcher paper, illustrating what they remember of the expedition.
2. T gives Ss time to reflect and discuss what they wish to include in the mural before they begin, and decide who will draw what. This discussion may be in the Ss own language if necessary.
3. Ss draw the mural and label all the items in it in the target language. The Ss may ask each other or the T for the vocabulary they don't know.
4. Ss then write short individual or group stories using the mural for reference. T may help if necessary.

Variations
   For additional vocabulary building, Ss can mimic individuals they may have depicted on the mural. T writes the new words on the blackboard for Ss to include in the mural, e.g., "A man fishing."

Special considerations
   If the class is too large, Ss can divide into smaller groups to draw several murals.

ACTIVITY 32

Hide and Seek with Prepositions
Level BI

Investment Ss imagine where to hide objects they have chosen in a picture. Other Ss try to locate them by asking questions.

Options
Grammar Prepositions, adjectives.
Vocabulary Words pertaining to houses and furnishings.

Materials Large-size pictures of houses, schools, furnished rooms, etc.

Procedure
1. T asks Ss to brainstorm names of all the items in the picture taped to the blackboard.
2. T draws lines out from the objects in the picture and writes identifying words on the blackboard.
3. T asks for a S to come forward, decide on an object, and mentally hide it somewhere in the picture.
4. The S tells classmates what the object is. Then the other Ss try to guess where it is hidden in the picture.
5. The S who guesses correctly gets to hide the next object.

Variations
With more advanced Ss, T can omit the first two steps.

Special considerations
Prepositions of place should be taught before this exercise.

ACTIVITY 33

Personality Capsule

Investment Ss write a short capsule about a person in a picture.

Options

Grammar Modals, adjectives, adverbs.

Culture What Ss observe in pictures is often based on culture-bound opinions; e.g., a picture of two men embracing might be interpreted differently by Ss from different cultures.

Materials Thought-provoking pictures of people that Ss or T brings to class.

Procedure
1. T shows pictures of a person to the class, e.g., a picture of a man holding his head.
2. T asks each S to write a few sentences (or a short story) about the person in the picture, describing what he's thinking, feeling, or what may have happened to him. T helps if needed.
3. T asks for volunteers to read their stories to the class.

Alternative procedure (for advanced Ss)
1. T asks Ss to brainstorm observations they make about a picture the T has furnished.
2. As Ss brainstorm, T or another S writes their observations on the blackboard.
3. T asks the class whether these are truly observations or opinions. Ss can discuss the differences between these two concepts.
4. Ss look at the list again and underline what they feel are true observations.
5. Ss and the T can discuss how observations and opinions can be culturally biased, e.g., picture of an American college student of the late sixties in ragged blue jeans might suggest that the student is poor. However, this is an opinion, since ragged jeans were the uniform of the late sixties college generation.

Variation
T asks someone who is unfamiliar to the Ss to make an impromptu visit to the class wearing unconventional clothes and performing unexplained actions. Class discusses observations and opinions after the person leaves.

Drawing the Students' Homes Level BIA

Investment   Each S draws a picture of his/her home for a class guessing game activity.

Options

Grammar   Possessive pronouns, modals, WH questions, *there is/there are*.

Vocabulary   Words pertaining to the home.

Theme   The home.

Culture   In a multi-national class Ss could discuss and compare the differences of the houses in their countries.

Materials   Ss' own drawing materials.

Procedure

1. T directs the Ss to draw pictures of their homes as detailed as they want for homework. They are not to show their pictures to other members of the class.
2. The following day the T collects the pictures and then passes each one out to another S. The T directs the Ss to write one descriptive sentence, on the strips of paper provided, about the pictures they have using the sentence, e.g., "It must be_____'s house, because . . ."
3. After the Ss have completed writing their sentences, the T posts each picture with the sentence under it in the front of the room.
4. The Ss in turn, pointing to the picture they wrote about, explain why they think that house belongs to a particular person in the class. Other Ss may contribute their observations.

Variations

Same exercises can be done with the Ss drawing their "dream house."

ACTIVITY **35**

Catalogue Shopping on a Limited Budget
Level BIA

Investment   Ss talk about and decide what they can buy with restricted funds from a catalogue.

Options
Grammar   Count and noncount nouns, comparatives, WH questions, past tense.

Vocabulary   Words used for shopping.

Theme   Shopping, gifts.

Culture   Ss can talk about appropriate gifts in their own culture for family, special occasions.

Materials   Department store catalogues or a catalogue made with pictures cut out from magazines, two sets of index cards, one listing buying situations, e.g., a birthday present for your father, a lamp for the bedroom; the other set of cards showing different amounts of money.

Procedure
1.   T puts the two sets of index cards on a table.
2.   Each S draws both a money card and a situation card.
3.   Ss working in small groups consult the catalogues to try to find the item they need for their situation, which will be limited by the amount of money they have, e.g., a present for Grandma for $8, furniture for the living room for $15.
4.   T should be available to explain new words to Ss when needed, and to serve as a financial adviser.
5.   After the Ss have selected the items they plan to buy, they "show and tell" the rest of the class.

Variations
Ss can write the new words found in the catalogue on the blackboard to be copied into their notebooks for later use in writing sentences.

Ss can report back to classmates on what they bought, using the past tense.

ACTIVITY **36**

Picture Interview Level BIA

Investment Ss assume the personalities of people in pictures and answer questions from the class in a simulated interview.

Options
Grammar WH and yes/no questions, verb+infinitive, adverbs, adjectives.
Theme Professions, family relationships.

Materials T or Ss provide pictures of interesting-looking people from the Ss' own or the target language culture.

Procedure
1. T places the pictures face down on a table and asks a S to select one of them.
2. The S shows the picture to the class and then silently decides on an identity to assume. The other Ss think of questions they would like to ask the character in the picture.
3. The S then takes on the identity representing the person in that picture, and answers the other Ss' questions appropriately.
4. The same procedure continues, with the other Ss taking on assumed identities.

Variations
     Ss can write a short paragraph or story about the character they assumed in the pictures.
     This can be in an interview format with Ss acting as newspaper or TV reporters.
     Ss in pairs can reconstruct the interview using reported speech.
     For beginning classes: 1. Ss could be given the pictures beforehand, so that they can prepare a short paragraph about the character. One at a time, Ss read their own paragraphs to the rest of the class before the interview takes place. 2. T shows the class a picture, then asks questions about it which can be answered with yes or no.

ACTIVITY 37

Picture Story

Level BIA

Investment Ss choose a picture to write a composite story about.

Options

Grammar   Verb tenses (general), modal perfects, logical connectors.

Culture   Pictures may reveal cultural insights that Ss can write about.

Theme   Any focus, e.g., mystery or love story.

Materials Pictures (provided by Ss or T) taken from magazines and mounted on construction paper. Butcher paper, felt markers.

Procedure

1. T puts out four or five pictures. Class selects one of them to write three or four sentences about.
2. The class breaks up into small groups. Each group writes its sentences as correctly as possible about the picture.
3. One representative at a time from each group writes its sentences on butcher paper or the blackboard.
4. When all the sentences are written up, T asks the Ss to reflect silently on the general transcript for about 5 minutes, to see whether there are any corrections or changes they would like to make.
5. Ss point out and correct any errors they note.
6. If any errors go unnoticed, T underlines them and asks Ss to look over those sentences again and try to correct them.
7. T asks Ss to return to their original groups and write composite stories about the pictures using sentences from the transcript. Ss read their stories aloud to the class or post them on the blackboard.

Variations

Advanced Ss can work on logical connectors, editing and condensing the story, or can write longer, more complicated stories.

Ss can act out their stories.

ACTIVITY 38

Story Sequence
from Unrelated Pictures

Level BIA

Investment   Ss select pictures to create an improvised story.

Options

Grammar   Any focus of teacher's choice, e.g., logical connectors, compounding, subordinates, verb tenses (general), word order.

Theme   T can preselect pictures to relate to a particular theme such as *the family*.

Materials   Pictures from magazines.

Procedure
1. T places pile of unrelated pictures face down on the table.
2. Ss divide into small groups. Each group takes three to five pictures.
3. Ss in each group sequence their pictures and write a story about them.
4. Each group reads its story to the rest of the class.

Variations

   To enhance investment, Ss may be asked to bring in their own pictures.

Special considerations

   It is important that the pictures be unrelated. This provides a more amusing challenge.

ACTIVITY 39

Travelogue

Investment   Ss create travel posters and describe them to the class.

Options

Grammar   Verbs: present tense for expressing future time, simple future, past tense, and present perfect; *there is/there are*; prepositions, asking questions.

Vocabulary   Words concerning times, places, and dates.

Theme   Vacation plans and travel.

Materials   Travel magazines provided by T or Ss, construction paper, scissors, scotch tape, paste.

Procedure
1. T explains that the Ss should put together a sequence of pictures showing travel plans, e.g., buying a ticket, taking a plane or boat, visiting national monuments.
2. T then tells the Ss to divide into pairs and select one or two travel magazines to cut out the pictures for their travel posters.
3. After the Ss have selected and arranged their pictures according to their trip schedule, they paste them onto large-sized construction paper.
4. Ss write captions for each picture, which include place, time, and date, e.g., "Arrive in Rome, September 5"; "Fly to Paris, September 20." T is available to help Ss if needed.
5. Each pair "shows and tells" the other Ss about its travel plans. The class may ask questions about the trip.

Variations

   Ss recount travel plans in the past tense, as if the trip had already taken place.

   Ss can write an imaginary journal about the trip.

   Ss discuss things they need to take along on the trip, e.g., passports, cameras, travelers' checks, special wardrobe.

   Ss discuss the steps for carrying out any of the travel plans, e.g., making plane or hotel reservations.

Using Pictures as a Diagnostic Tool — Level BIA

Investment   To diagnose the Ss' knowledge of the target language, T has the Ss describe the pictures he/she has provided.

Options

Grammar   General: indicates the Ss' knowledge of the target language grammar and vocabulary.

Theme   Pictures can focus on a theme, e.g., cities, people, food, clothing.

Materials   About 7 to 15 magazine pictures which are rich in content. The number of pictures depends upon the class level. If desired, these can be centered around a specific theme.

Procedure

1. T spreads the pictures face up on the floor or on a large table and asks the Ss to study them carefully for a few minutes.
2. T collects the pictures and mixes them up. T then puts them all, except one, back down for the Ss to look at.
3. T then asks the Ss to describe the picture that the T is still holding. They should try to remember as many details as possible. T can give some information or ask very specific questions to help prod their memories.
4. Ss continue describing the pictures as specifically as possible.

Special considerations

Pictures may be simpler in content for beginners.

ACTIVITY 41

Which Way?

Investment   Ss draw a map of a town and give directions to one another on how to get from place to place.

Options
Grammar   Imperatives, prepositions, *there is/there are,* asking questions.
Vocabulary   Words pertaining to direction giving and town layout.
Theme   Giving directions.

Materials   Large sheets of butcher paper, felt markers, Cuisenaire rods, toy cars (optional).

Procedure
1.   T divides the class into groups of not more than ten Ss.
2.   Each group gathers around a large piece of butcher paper placed either on the floor or on a big table.
3.   T tells Ss that each group is to draw a map of a downtown area, which should include city blocks, main streets, etc.
4.   Each group then plans and draws their map on the butcher paper using felt markers.
5.   Each S silently plans how to direct another S within the group to a specific destination in the town.
6.   A S (S1) then gives another S (S2) in the same group the directions for getting from one place to another.
7.   S2 uses a Cuisenaire rod to represent a person following S1's directions. Procedure continues until all the Ss have given and followed directions.

Variations
   More advanced Ss can ask one another how to get from place to place, and respondents must give spontaneous directions.
   Rods may be used to represent cars. Consulting the map, one S at a time assumes the role of a driving instructor telling an S driver where to go.
   Ready-made maps of cities can be used for this exercise if they are scaled large enough.

ACTIVITY 42

Picture Narrative

Investment Ss in small groups select a picture and write a story about it.

Options
Grammar WH and yes/no questions, any grammar focus of teacher's choice.

Theme Any theme, e.g., family, home, shops, travel.

Culture Ss can compare family relationships in target language and their own cultures.

Materials Pictures from magazines.

Procedures
1. Ss divide into small groups. Each group selects one picture and writes a narrative about it. T helps with vocabulary and grammar if necessary, or Ss may use dictionaries.
2. A spokesman from each group reads the completed story to the class.
3. After the S has read the story, he/she or other group members ask the rest of the class comprehension questions.
4. Then the class questions one another about the narrative.
5. Other members of the class retell the story in their own words.

Variations
Ss can act out each others' narratives.

ACTIVITY 43

Guess It Right

Investment S volunteers describe pictures to their classmates in an exercise to test memory and powers of discrimination.

Options

Grammar *There is/there are,* adjectives and adverbs, prepositions, WH and yes/no questions.

Theme Any theme, e.g., towns, people.

Culture Pictures may illustrate a typical activity in target language or Ss' own culture, e.g., holiday festivities.

Materials Four large-sized pictures from magazines. For each of these pictures there should be one or two other pictures closely resembling them in subject matter and composition.

Procedure
1. T puts four or five pictures face down on a center table and asks an equal number of Ss to select one each. Ss do not show their pictures to the class or one another.
2. T tells the Ss to study their own pictures carefully for a few minutes.
3. One by one, Ss describe their pictures to the class.
4. After each S has described his/her picture, the class asks questions to get a more precise idea of it.
5. T collects the pictures and then mixes them up with the set of closely similar pictures which he/she has held in reserve.
6. T tapes all the pictures to the blackboard in random order.
7. Ss look over the pictures and decide which were the exact ones described.
8. T asks the Ss the reasons for their choices.
9. Ss then show the pictures they had described to the class.

Variations
    T can do this activity with small groups of Ss using postcards or photographs instead of large pictures.

ACTIVITY 44

Personality Poster Level IA

Investment Ss bring in pictures to make a "personality" poster representing themselves.

Options
Grammar Verb + infinitive, gerunds, verb tenses (general).

Vocabulary Adjectives pertaining to personality traits.

Materials Pictures Ss have cut out from magazines showing their favorite activities and/or personality traits. Construction paper or poster board.

Procedure
1. Ss bring pictures to class, or select from other ones the T has provided.
2. With these pictures, Ss make up posters which best represent their own characteristics and interests.
3. Ss mount the pictures on colored construction paper or poster board. They then may label or put captions under the pictures, e.g., "I love to dance." T may help if needed.
4. Each S presents own poster to the class and explains it.

Variations
Ss can describe each others' posters.

Posters can be mixed up and the class can guess whose poster is whose and why.

Posters can be made at home.

ACTIVITY 45

Picture Memory Game

Level IA

Investment Ss select pictures which they question one another about.

Options
Grammar Count/noncount nouns, adjectives, present progressive, indefinite pronouns, relative clauses.

Vocabulary Words pertaining to physical surroundings, e.g., landscape, furniture.

Materials Pictures with many different items or actions.

Procedure
1. T divides class into two groups.
2. T tells each group to select a picture and carefully study all the details in it for 3 minutes. Groups then exchange their pictures.
3. Group A, looking at Group B's picture, questions them very specifically about it, e.g., "How many apple trees are there in this picture?" "Is there a little girl in the garden?"
4. T keeps score on the blackboard. Any wrong answers count against the group.
5. Groups reverse. Group B then questions Group A.

Variations
The groups can compose true-false questions about the pictures.
Each group writes sentences about its picture, after it has been removed.
If the picture has people in it, it can be used for practicing restrictive relative clauses.

ACTIVITY **46**

Creating a Small Town
Level IA

Investment Ss discuss and draw an imaginary target language community which includes the homes and businesses of people they think would live there.

Options

Grammar Modals, *there is/there are,* WH and yes/no questions, imperatives and prepositions.

Vocabulary Words referring to houses and town layouts.

Culture Ss discuss and reflect on special features of the target language community.

Materials Butcher paper, felt markers, Cuisenaire rods (optional).

Procedure
1. T puts a large piece of butcher paper on the floor or on a table, and tells the Ss they are going to create a typical target language community.
2. Ss brainstorm all the important landmarks and buildings they think may be found in the community. T lists these on the blackboard, and makes further suggestions if necessary.
3. Ss then discuss and draw up a town plan, using the buildings, landmarks, etc., listed on the blackboard.
4. Ss talk about what kind of individuals are likely to live in the typical community, e.g., mayor, banker, drunkard, rich widow. T lists these on the blackboard.
5. Ss choose which characters they would each like to role-play and adopt names for these persons. T notes these down as a basis for a future exercise.
6. Ss then discuss among themselves the types of houses and places of business where these people would be most likely to live and work, and draw them on the map.

Variations
Lesson can focus on prepositions of place, direction giving, etc.
For continuation the following day, T writes up a problem for each person role playing, which necessitates their interacting in a "cocktail party"* situation.

---

*See activity 63.

Ss can make up brief skits based on the characters they have chosen.

T has Ss construct a community from their own culture first, if they are unfamiliar with the makeup of a target language community. Ss could then go out in pairs to interview people from the target language culture, to gather information about the layout of their communities, so they can then draw one in class.

Ss construct whay they think would be an ideal community, high school, college, etc.

V Rod Activities

ACTIVITY 47

Back-to-Back Directions   Level BIA

Investment Ss give and follow directions for building or drawing a construction.

Options
Grammar   Prepositions, imperatives, comparatives.
Vocabulary   Colors, sizes, shapes.
Theme   Giving and understanding directions.

Materials Cuisenaire rods, puzzles, Tinker Toys, paper.

Procedure
1. Ss seat themselves in pairs back to back.
2. In each pair, S1 makes a construction and then tells S2 as specifically as possible how to duplicate it, e.g., "Make a square with green rods." "In the middle of the square, put a small white rod."
3. If T decides to allow questioning, S2 may query S1 if the directions are unclear.
4. When S2 completes the replica, he/she turns around and compares it with S1's to see if they are identical.
5. Procedure is reversed. S2 makes a structure and gives directions to S1.

Variations
For advanced Ss, more complicated constructions can be built with Tinker Toys or rods.

Ss can give directions on drawing geometric figures.

ACTIVITY 48

A Day in the Park

Level BIA

Investment   Using their imagination, Ss describe the layout of a public park and the people visiting it.

Options
Grammar   Prepositions, verb tenses (general), adjectives and adverbs.

Vocabulary   Words pertaining to park layout.

Culture   Ss may compare typical parks in the target language culture and their own.

Materials   Cuisenaire rods.

Procedure
1.   Ss sit in a circle on the floor or around a table.
2.   In the center of the circle, T silently makes a representation of a park that has benches, trees, fountains, etc., using rods of different sizes and colors.
3.   Following this, Ss guess what the construction is. When they realize it is a park, they identify what the rods represent.
4.   T can put a time focus on the lesson by telling the Ss to talk about yesterday, this morning, every day, or tomorrow in the park.
5.   The T takes a rod and gives it a name, e.g., Mr. Green, and silently guides him as he performs various actions in the park, e.g., sitting on a bench, drinking from a water fountain. Ss describe what Mr. Green is doing in the verb tense indicated in Step 4.
6.   The T continues, using rod representations for other people while Ss tell what is happening.
7.   The T lets the Ss take over the maneuvering of the rods, continuing the narrative with other Ss, and conducting dialogues between people in the park, etc.

Variations
More advanced Ss can perform all the steps in the procedure, instead of the T.

Ss write individual or group stories about interesting people in the park.

ACTIVITY 49

Do as I Say

Investment   Ss instruct one another to make a specific construction with rods.

Options
Grammar   Imperatives, present progressive tense, adjectives.

Materials   Cuisenaire rods.

Procedure
1. For demonstration the T gives instruction to various Ss one at a time on how to make a certain construction with rods, e.g., "Put the green rod on the red one." "Now put a blue rod perpendicular to them."
2. The roles reverse; individual Ss then take turns giving the T directions on building a construction.
3. Following this Ss can then practice in pairs or in small groups repeating similar instructions or making up new ones of their own.

Variations
   Ss draw cards from a box with the directions for making a construction which they can do themselves or tell other Ss how to do.
   For more advanced Ss T silently makes a more complicated design with the rods. One S then instructs the T on how to make the same construction again. T follows S's orders exactly. The S must be very specific, since directions are easily misunderstood.

ACTIVITY 50

The Five-Story Building

Level BIA

Investment Ss plan and construct a building with Cuisenaire rods.

Options
Grammar Prepositions, WH questions, *there is/there are,* modals.
Vocabulary Buildings and professions, ordinal numbers.
Theme Professions, buildings.

Materials Cuisenaire rods.

Procedure
1. T puts the rods on the table. Lays one rod down horizontally and says: "first floor."
2. T places another rod horizontally on top of the first rod and waits for Ss to respond with "second floor."
3. Ss continue construction, saying which floor each rod represents. T stops them at the fifth floor.
4. T asks Ss which offices and shops are on the first floor. Ss state what they think might be there. T writes words on the blackboard.
5. T then rebuilds first floor with different-colored rods, representing the places the Ss had mentioned.
6. Ss continue building, saying which offices and shops the rods represent on each floor. When Ss have finished, they should have a multi-colored 5-story building.

Variations
Beginning Ss can bring in pictures of offices and shops. They can be used as references for the offices in the rod building.
Ss can talk about occupants of each office, as a focus on occupations.

Special considerations
T will need to teach the ordinal numbers before this exercise.

ACTIVITY 51

Tell and Show

Investment Ss describe places of special importance to them, e.g., their home, a village square, a town they have visited. Each S should choose a place unfamiliar to the other Ss.

Options
Grammar	*There is/there are,* simple present, past tenses, prepositions.
Vocabulary	Words concerning houses and town layouts.
Theme	Homes, towns, past experiences (auto accidents, etc.).
Culture	Ss talk about a place meaningful to them, either in their own country or anywhere they have ever been.

Materials Cuisenaire rods and an *empty* table top.

Procedure
1. One S at a time chooses a place to describe to the T one sentence at a time. With each sentence S puts one or more Cuisenaire rods into place to represent what has been said. S may speak in the target language, native language, or some combination of the two. The T gives "understanding responses" after each sentence in the target language.
2. When S has finished, T summarizes the whole as if asking for verification of his/her own factual understanding and memory.
3. When S1 has completed the description, other Ss take turns pointing to the rods and telling one fact per turn of things they remember from the account to show that they were listening, interested, and have understood.
4. While individual Ss are summarizing, the T repeats the utterance in correct form to S1. The T's manner is conversational, *not* pedagogical. Errors are not pointed out. No questions are permitted in this phase, only summarizing.
5. The observers now may ask S1 questions about the description to find out more information. The T's role here is the same as in Step 4.
6. The same procedure (which takes about 20 to 30 minutes in a small class) can be repeated another day with a different student.
7. Material generated in this way may then be used as basis for any of many kinds of practice: reading, writing, dictation, etc.

Special considerations
   The T communicates directly only with the S who is describing his/her place. In this way corrections of the observers' statements are indirect.

ACTIVITY 52

Rod Figures

Investment Ss make rod representations of themselves to describe to their classmates and the T.

Options
Grammar   Simple present, adjectives.

Vocabulary   Colors, parts of the body.

Theme   Personal identity.

Materials   Cuisenaire rods or Tinker Toys

Procedure
1. T puts a large pile of rods on the table or the floor.
2. T instructs Ss to make representations of themselves with the rods. They may be as simple or elaborate as the Ss wish.
3. When the Ss have finished, T asks for a volunteer to display his/her rod image. Other Ss then try to guess and explain why it was represented in such a way.
4. When Ss have finished, the volunteer explains the rod design.
5. This procedure continues until all Ss have displayed and explained their rod figures.

ACTIVITY 53

Basic Sentence Patterns with Rods   Level IA

Investment Ss create their own sentences according to a pattern represented by rods, paper clips, and cardboard dots.

Options
Grammar   Word order, logical connectors, relative clauses, punctuation.

Materials Cuisenaire rods, paper clips for commas, cardboard dots for periods.

Procedure
1. Ss sit in a circle around a table or on the floor.
2. T lays down one long blue rod, putting a white dot (period) at the end. T models a simple declarative sentence, e.g., "Charlie has good taste."
3. T asks Ss to come up with their own sentences following the same pattern.
4. T then sets up another pattern consisting of a blue rod, paper clip, a small white rod, and another blue rod. This represents two independent sentences connected by a conjunction.
5. T without modeling waits to see if the Ss can come up with a sentence that fits this second rod pattern. If the Ss can't, T gives one example, e.g., "Charlie has good taste, but he doesn't taste good." T then lets the Ss continue giving their own examples.
6. T continues with more complicated sentence pattern, using the rods to illustrate structures the Ss have already studied (see the sample).
7. Ss can then write an original paragraph using all the sentence patterns represented.

Variations
For an advanced class, the Ss can make their own representations of the sentence patterns they know with the rods without the T's help.
Ss can change these statements into questions using the rods.

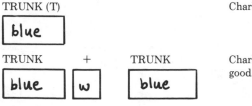

TRUNK (T)   Charlie has good taste.

TRUNK   +   TRUNK   Charlie has good taste, but he doesn't taste good.

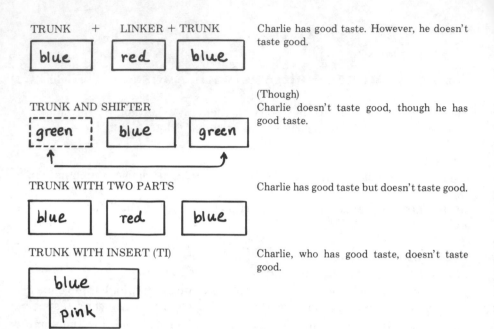

TRUNK   +   LINKER + TRUNK

| blue | red | blue |

Charlie has good taste. However, he doesn't taste good.

TRUNK AND SHIFTER

| green | blue | green |

(Though)
Charlie doesn't taste good, though he has good taste.

TRUNK WITH TWO PARTS

| blue | red | blue |

Charlie has good taste but doesn't taste good.

TRUNK WITH INSERT (TI)

| blue |
| pink |

Charlie, who has good taste, doesn't taste good.

ACTIVITY 54

Building a Class Dream House   Level IA

Investment   Ss create own dream house—variation of Tell and Show.*

Options

Grammar   Prepositions of place, *there is/there are,* present tense, other/another, WH questions.

Vocabulary Words referring to the home.

Culture   Ss compare an ideal home in their own and target language community.

Materials   Cuisenaire rods, felt markers, butcher paper, toy furniture (optional).

Procedure

1. Depending on class size, Ss remain in one group or divide into smaller units for this exercise.

2. T puts the rods on the floor or a table and explains to the class that they are to discuss, agree upon, and lay out the floor plan of an ideal house. The plan should be on a large enough scale to allow for placement of furniture represented by rods or toy furniture.

3. After Ss have finished constructing and furnishing the house, S1 selects a room to describe to the T. As S1 describes the room, the T listens carefully and then summarizes what S has said after every three or four sentences. This summary can be an indirect way of correcting the S's linguistic mistakes. Other Ss observe but do *not* comment.

4. For purposes of reinforcement, other Ss in the group then describe the same room back to S1. T may summarize their statements in the same manner as with S1.

5. Ss can then question S1 about the room.

6. Procedure continues with other Ss taking turns describing the other rooms to the T. T summarizes while the other Ss observe and then later question.

Special considerations

If the class is small enough (seven or eight Ss), T can work with the whole group. In larger classes T can model the exercise with one group and then ask more advanced Ss or teacher aides to help with the other groups.

---

* See activity 51.

VI Tape Recorder/Transcripts

ACTIVITY 55

Chain Story

Investment Ss contribute sentences to a group chain story which is recorded.

Options

Grammar   Any focus of teacher's choice, e.g., logical connectors, verb tenses (general), word order.

Theme   Ss can decide on any theme, e.g., school, home, a mystery.

Materials Tape recorder, butcher paper (optional).

Procedure
1. Ss form circle around tape recorder.
2. S1 makes up sentence to begin the story. If the grammar is incorrect, the T restates it correctly. When the S is satisfied with the sentence, he/she records it.
3. S2 repeats S1's sentence and adds another original sentence to the story.
4. T restates S2's original sentence if correction is needed. When S2 is satisfied with this sentence, he/she tapes it.
5. The same procedure is followed by all Ss in the circle, each repeating all previous Ss' sentences, but taping only their own.
6. T plays back the complete story.

Variations

A transcript of the chain story may be written on the blackboard or on butcher paper.

For more advanced groups, repetition of Ss' previous sentences may not be necessary.

ACTIVITY 56

General Procedure for
Language Taping
Level BIA

Investment   Ss create their own language lesson by saying whatever they want to on the tape recorder.

Options
Grammar   Any grammatical structure the Ss come up with.

Theme   Ss may pick a special theme to talk about.

Materials   Tape recorder with microphone, blank tape.

Procedure
1. T has Ss sit in a small circle around a tape recorder that is placed on a table or chair. All the Ss should be close enough to the recorder so they can reach the microphone without getting up.
2. T gives the following explanation of the taping session:
   a. Ss will record in the target language for a total period of 5 to 10 minutes.
   b. Taking turns, Ss may say anything they want to onto the tape.
   c. No S is required to speak if he/she doesn't want to.
3. For the first taping session, the T explains how to operate the tape recorder microphone. The Ss can then practice using the microphone by saying their names onto the recorder.
4. Ss then proceed with the taping. One S at a time takes the microphone, pushes the "on" button, and says whatever he/she wants to. When the utterance is completed, S turns off the microphone and places it back on the recorder. The T does *not* correct the S's utterance.
5. After the taping session is over, the T gets "feedback"* from the Ss on how they felt about the taping. T listens attentively and then summarizes after each S speaks.
6. T plays back the Ss' recording uninterrupted.
7. T follows up with posttaping transcript session (see activity 57).

Special considerations
   It is important for the S to fell secure. The T can help with this by:
   a. Not requiring any S to speak if he/she doesn't want to.
   b. Not correcting or restating the S's statement.

---

*See Guide to Terminology and Abbreviations.

c. Asking the Ss to put the microphone back in the center when they are finished speaking, not passing it from one S to another, thereby making Ss feel obligated to speak.

d. Always including a "feedback" session, so that the Ss have an opportunity to express any problems they may be having with the lesson. T should give reassuring and understanding responses that help the Ss feel more secure.

During the first few taping sessions the Ss might be self-conscious; so they may say only things they are absolutely sure of. After a few sessions, though, the Ss usually become more spontaneous and are willing to take the risk of not always being correct.

ACTIVITY 57

Posttaping Transcript Session

Investment   A S or the T transcribes the taped lesson so the class can reflect on and correct it.

Options
Grammar   Any grammatical structure the Ss come up with; for example, see Step 6 for suggestion about adverbs of manner.

Materials   Felt markers, butcher paper.

Procedure
1. After a completed taping session, T asks for a S volunteer to play back the tape, stopping at the end of each sentence, so that the T or another S can write the sentences on butcher paper posted in the front of the room.
2. T then gives the Ss about 5 minutes to look silently at the completed transcript and see whether they have any questions about the grammar or vocabulary.
3. At the end of 5 minutes, the T asks the Ss if there are any changes or corrections they want to make. If so, the T makes the corrections and changes suggested.
4. If any mistakes go undetected, the T underlines or circles them. The T asks the class if they feel they need to make any other changes.
5. T then asks the Ss if there are any parts of the transcript which are unclear or they are unsure of. T underlines whatever the Ss mention. This will help the T in planning future lessons based on the Ss' needs.
6. T tells Ss to close their eyes and listen silently as T reads the corrected transcript through about 3 times. The T reads it differently each time, e.g., slowly, normally, happily, or reads it to classical music (see activity 60).
7. Ss copy the transcript into their notebooks.
8. Ss can then practice the material on the transcript in pairs by doing any of the exercises in activity 58.
9. T then has another "feedback session" about the lesson.

ACTIVITY 58

Transcript Follow-up Exercises Level BIA

Suggestions

1. *Unfinished sentences:* Using 3×5 cards, T writes half of a sentence taken from the transcript on one side of the card and the other half on the reverse side. T gives a set of these cards to Ss in pairs.

   As one S holds up a card, the other S reads the first half and then tries to fill in the second half of the sentence as he remembers it from the transcript. The S holding the card can look at the back to see if it's correct.

2. *Erasure technique:* T writes the sentences from the transcript on the blackboard and asks one S to read them back. T then erases one word from the first sentence and has another S read the sentence back, filling in the missing word. T continues erasing words from the sentences and having different Ss read a sentence each time a word is erased. This procedure goes on until there are no words left on the blackboard.

3. *Dictation:* T dictates sentences from the transcript.

4. *Scrambled sentences:* T or Ss may make up scrambled sentences from the transcript (see activity 7).

5. *Transcript story:* Ss can create a story using sentences from the transcript. They can follow this up by doing a Cloze exercise.

6. *Dialogues:* Ss in pairs can create dialogues from the transcript to be performed in class.

7. *New sentences:* Ss may make up new sentences or questions from the transcript, or rewrite original sentences using other verb tenses.

8. *Transcript recall:* Ss copy the transcript into their notebooks. They then practice in pairs, alternating reading their sentences to each other in the order in which they occur on the transcript. Then as one S reads a sentence, the other S tries to remember and say the following sentence, etc.

ACTIVITY **59**

Lessons of the Week in Review

Investment Ss create their own dialogues from review of the week's lessons.

Options
Grammar Review.
Vocabulary Review.

Materials Tape recorder with microphone, classical music tape, blank tape.

Procedure
1. T says sentences from the week's lessons to classical music for 10 to 15 minutes following the procedure outlined in activity 60.
2. T then puts a blank tape into the tape recorder. Ss are invited to tape sentences using the same structures that were used during the listening session. One S at a time records one or two sentences. After S has spoken the sentence, the microphone is replaced so other Ss can tape any sentences they come up with.
3. T plays the newly taped sentences back for Ss to listen to.
4. A S plays back one sentence at a time, as the T writes them up on butcher paper with *no* corrections.
5. T gives the Ss 5 to 10 minutes to reflect on their transcript and to make any changes they see fit.
6. Ss then break up into pairs to create a short dialogue using sentences and words from the transcript.
7. The S pairs practice and then perform their dialogues for the class.

ACTIVITY **60**

Music to Remember by   Level BIA

Investment T uses S-created sentences for this listening exercise.

Options
Grammar Any grammar focus of teacher's choice.

Materials Tape recorder, tapes of classical music, e.g., Beethoven's Fifth Symphony or Chopin are especially recommended.

Procedure
1. T tells the Ss that they will be listening to music while T is speaking. The Ss should visualize the T's sentences as they enjoy the music in a relaxed state with their eyes closed.
2. T plays the music while saying sentences from the day's lesson which need reinforcement. The T should speak in a soothing voice to the mood and rhythm of the music.
3. T repeats the series of sentences two or three times. This listening period might last for 15 to 20 minutes.
4. Following the music, the T should allow the Ss to reflect silently on the sentences for about 5 minutes.
5. T then asks the Ss to repeat any of the sentences, if they wish.

Variations
    T can do dialogues or stories to the music, introduce vocabulary with pictures, or present new structures.
    T can use this as review of the week's lessons.

Special considerations
    Classical music with an andante tempo works best with this exercise. T should practice this activity before trying it in class.

VII   Theater Techniques

ACTIVITY 61

In What Manner?   Level BI

Investment   Ss decide on actions and how to perform them.

Options
Grammar   Imperatives and adverbs of manner.

Materials   None.

Procedure
1. T asks S to leave the room briefly.
2. While the S is outside, the remaining Ss choose an action that they will do after he returns, e.g., *walk across the room.*
3. The S comes back into the room and without knowing the action the other Ss have chosen, gives them an adverb of manner, e.g., stupidly, sweetly, happily.
4. The class must perform the action according to the adverb of manner indicated.
5. The same procedure follows, with other Ss going out of the room.

Special considerations
   With a beginning class it may be necessary for the T to brainstorm all possible adverbs of manner before proceeding with the activity.
   The fact that the activity may not match up well with the adverb can make this an amusing exercise.

ACTIVITY 62

Amnesia

Investment Ss discover their own assumed identities by questioning one another.

Options

Grammar Verb tenses (general), WH and yes/no questions, adjectives, adverbs.

Vocabulary Professions.

Theme Currently famous people, family members, historical figures, etc.

Materials Enough 3×5 index cards with names of persons printed on them for every member of the class, straight pins.

Procedure
1. T explains to Ss that they are each suffering from amnesia and don't know who they are. T then pins an index card with a name of a famous person on it to each S's back. Ss must *not* reveal each other's identities.
2. T tells Ss that in order to discover their own identities they must mingle with the other Ss for about 15 minutes and ask questions about themselves, e.g., "Where do I come from?" "What do I do?" "What do I look like?" They must not ask the other Ss directly who they are.
3. When each S figures out own identity, he/she neither reveals it nor confirms it with the other Ss or the T.
4. When the time is up, Ss form a circle and reveal who they think they are.

Variations

Ss talk about clues which helped them guess their identities.

Ss describe other famous characters they met in the course of the game.

Ss have extemporaneous dialogues with one another taking on their assumed personalities.

ACTIVITY 63

Cocktail Party

Level BIA

Investment Ss make up their own conversations based on imaginary situations and personalities who are all interrelated in some way.

Options
Grammar   Any grammar focus of teacher's choice, WH questions, register.

Theme   Family gatherings—relationships discovered; neighborhood party—local gossip, entanglements; Caribbean cruise or Greyhound bus trip—strangers discover how their lives are intertwined.

Procedure
1. T passes out cards with brief bio-sketch identities that Ss will assume (see sample).
2. Ss proceed to find out how their lives are connected by meeting and talking with as many people as possible in the group.
3. After the "cocktail party" is over the Ss can explain to the T how their relationships are connected.

Variations
More advanced Ss can make up their own bio-sketches, which T can then use to create the entanglements.

T can bring in wine or soft drinks and food, and make it a more lifelike cocktail party.

Special considerations
In all "cocktail party" situations the students must discover what relationships exist between themselves and other characters. Therefore, all situations must be ones in which a variety of people are gathered together for some reason. Their lives must be quite interwoven. Each bio-sketch card should relate the card bearer to someone else in the scenario (see sample).

Sample   This is an example of a very basic "cocktail party" exercise. The focus here is on vocabulary of the family. Each S is given a slip of paper with one of the following biographical items:

1. Your name is Paul Benton. You are 52 years old. You are married and have three children.
2. Your name is Anne Benton. You are 45 years old. You are married to Paul Benton. You have three children.

3. Your name is Jim Benton. You are 21 years old. You have one brother and one sister. Your mother is Anne Benton.

4. Your name is Joe Benton. You are 21 years old. You have one brother and one sister. Your mother is Anne Benton.

5. Your name is Kathy Benton. You are 18 years old. You are the youngest child of Paul and Anne Benton.

6. Your name is Edward Benton. You are 49 years old. You have one son. You also have one brother who is three years older than you.

7. Your name is Barbara Benton. You are 47 years old. You are married to Edward Benton. Your only son Bill is 18 years old.

8. Your name is Bill Benton. You are 18 years old. You are an only child.

9. Your name is Lester Benton. You are 79 years old. You have two sons, Paul and Edward.

10. Your name is Grace Benton. You are 76 years old. Your husband is Lester Benton. You have two sons and four grandchildren.

Conversations
of an Eraser and Pencil

Level BIA

Investment   Ss create conversations between inanimate objects.

Options

Grammar   WH questions, negative and affirmative statements, modals, adverbials.

Materials   Any materials T or Ss wish to bring to class or objects in the classroom.

Procedure

1. T tells Ss to divide into pairs and decide which objects will conduct a conversation or interview with each other, e.g., pencil and pencil sharpener, eraser with blackboard, etc.
2. Ss then extemporaneously act and speak to each other like the objects they have chosen.
3. The other Ss in the class try to guess the objects in the dialogues.

Variations

Ss write dialogues for the objects.

ACTIVITY 65

Once More with Feeling

Investment   Ss write sentences and indicate how they should be read by their classmates.

Options
Pronunciation   Stress and intonation.

Materials   3×5 index cards, two boxes to hold index cards.

Procedure
1. Ss brainstorm* possible emotions, e.g., anger, happiness, sadness. T writes them on blackboard.
2. T asks each S to write a sentence on an index card. Sentences may have a special focus, e.g., commands, questions.
3. While the Ss are writing their sentences, the T copies the emotions from the blackboard onto separate index cards.
4. T puts the sentence cards in one box and the emotion cards in another.
5. S1 draws a sentence card and an emotion card and reads the sentence as the emotion card dictates.
6. Other Ss try to guess which emotion S1 is trying to portray.
7. Procedure continues until all Ss have had a chance to read.

---

*See Guide to Terminology and Abbreviations.

ACTIVITY 66

An "Operation"* Level BIA

Investment Ss decide on and perform a logically sequenced activity common in the target language culture or their own.

Options

Grammar Imperatives, two-word verbs, modals.

Vocabulary Focus on vocabulary needed for a particular "operation."

Theme Following directions, e.g., writing and posting a letter, using a pay telephone, etc.

Culture Culturally related activity may be demonstrated, e.g., the Japanese tea ceremony.

Materials Dependent on the type of "operation."

Procedure

1. T first demonstrates and then has Ss perform all the steps of a simple "operation" (see sample).
2. T has Ss brainstorm other types of activities that can be made into an "operation."
3. Ss pick one of these activities to make into an "operation" and brainstorm all the steps to carry it out. T writes these on the blackboard.
4. Ss then look over their suggested steps to see if they need to rephrase them using more accurate language. T can supply missing vocabulary if necessary.
5. Ss put the steps of the activity in a proper sequence and then limit it to about eight steps. Ss can then copy the steps into their notebooks.
6. T and Ss then perform the steps of the "operation" as explained on the sample.

Eating in a Restaurant ("Operation" Sample)

Materials Table, chairs, menu, check, money.

---

*See Guide to Terminology and Abbreviations.

Procedure

1. T models the entire chain of statements and accompanying actions.
   (a) find a table, (b) sit down, (c) look at the menu, (d) call the waiter/waitress, (e) order the meal, (f) eat the meal, (g) ask for the check, (h) pay waiter/waitress, cashier.
2. The T goes through the chain again to check Ss' comprehension.
3. The Ss perform the actions in response to directions of the T.
4. Ss give directions to the teacher, who carries them out.
5. The Ss give directions to each other.

Variations

1. The T may do the "operation" again (or at a later date) within a different tense context.
2. In advanced classes, as the Ss perform the actions the T can interrupt with questions in a different tense.
   Jean, pick up the _____ .
   What did you do?
   What are you going to do next?
   Have you _____ ed?
3. The T may introduce various request forms.
   Could you _____ ?
   Would you mind _____ ?
   _____ , would you please?
4. The T can introduce various modals and infinitive forms.
   In order to _____ , you must _____ .
   To _____ , you have to _____ .
5. The T can have Ss write the operation as a set of instructions or a paragraph describing a sequence of events.

ACTIVITY 67

Pantomime to Words

Investment   Ss in groups make up pantomimes to present to the class, which will be subsequently written into a story.

Options

Grammar   Any focus of teacher's choice, e.g., past tense.

Theme   Ss may decide on a theme before beginning the activity.

Culture   Ss can pantomime a typical activity in the target language culture or their own.

Materials   Dittos and paper.

Procedure

1.   T tells the Ss to divide into groups to create short pantomimes, and allows time for Ss to practice them.
2.   Ss then present their pantomimes. While they are performing, T takes notes to use in making up stories for a reading lesson.
3.   After each group has completed its pantomime, members ask observers questions about their skit.
4.   Following the class, the T writes up stories about the pantomimes and mimeographs them so each group has copies of its story.
5.   The next day T reads the stories to the Ss, and then follows each one up with very general comprehension questions.
6.   T passes out to each group copies of its own story which they will then read silently and discuss. T helps with vocabulary if needed.
7.   Each group then writes comprehension questions about its story for another group to answer.
8.   Groups exchange and read each others' stories and answer the questions. Stories and questions are then returned to the original groups for correction.

Variations

The groups act out each others' pantomimes.

ACTIVITY **68**

A Plane Trip

Investment   Ss converse freely during stopovers on a guided fantasy plane trip.

Options
Grammar   Review of verb tenses.
Theme   Plane trip, introductions, etiquette.

Materials   Chairs for airplane seats, tape recorder, music, index cards with fictional identities.

Procedure
1. T gives each S an index card with S's new identity and profession written on it. (These identities can be of well-known personalities with exciting careers in the target language culture.) T then introduces S to the class, e.g., "I would like you to meet John Travolta, the famous actor."
2. T directs the Ss to arrange the chairs as they would be on an airplane.
3. T tells the Ss to board the plane. After boarding, the T assumes the role of the pilot and describes to the passengers the sights below. Music can be played to help create the mood of the place they are going to visit.
4. The pilot then briefs the passengers on the first stopover and the people they are going to meet, e.g., "We are going to land in Hollywood, the home of many famous movie stars." "When you meet people here, enunciate very clearly, because clear diction is important in the entertainment world."
5. Ss then get off the plane for the brief stopover where they introduce themselves to each other and converse using clear diction.
6. The pilot announces that the passengers should reboard. After they have boarded, the pilot asks them how they enjoyed Hollywood, whether they met any interesting people, etc. The plane then flies on to another destination.
7. The plane makes three more stopovers, with the pilot giving separate briefings for each place, e.g., New York City, where the Ss must talk loudly because of the noise; on The Isle of Sark they must whisper because it's a very quiet place; in London they will be dancing and meeting people in a discotheque. During these stopovers, they continue meeting and talking with one another.

8. After the trip is over, the Ss in pairs or groups discuss highlights of their travels.
9. The Ss then write short passages about the place they enjoyed the most and some of the interesting people they met. These can then be posted on the bulletin board for the others to read.

Variations

Beginning Ss can focus on introductions and occupations only.

For verb tense review the Ss can speak in a different tense for each stopover, e.g., the pilot could say, "The people in Hollywood are only interested in talking about tomorrow, or the future."

Special considerations

T should have music that fits the mood of each stopover.

Stopovers shouldn't be much longer than 5 minutes.

ACTIVITY 69

Telephoning for Information Level BIA

Investment   Ss create own scenario for getting information by phone.

Options
Grammar   WH and yes/no questions, modals, present and future tenses, reported speech, verb + infinitive.
Vocabulary   Words needed to make travel arrangements or appointments.
Theme   Travel schedules, making appointments, etc.

Materials   Toy or dummy phones, butcher paper, and felt markers.

Procedure
1. Ss think of possible situations involving getting information or making appointments by phone. T lists these on the blackboard.
2. Ss decide on one situation from the list to investigate, and brainstorm possible questions they would need to ask. T writes these questions on the blackboard or butcher paper as said, including the errors.
3. T asks Ss to look at their questions, decide whether they are worded correctly, and revise if necessary.
4. T then underlines any undetected errors in the transcript, and asks the Ss to reexamine and correct them if they can. T can help if needed.
5. Ss give possible responses to their questions which the T writes on the blackboard.
6. Ss correct the responses as explained in Steps 3 and 4.
7. Ss break up into pairs to write dialogues using the questions and answers written on the blackboard.
8. Each pair performs its dialogue for the class, using the phone.

Variations
   Ss are assigned to call the T at home to find out the homework.
   T assumes the role of the person telephoned, e.g., ticket agent, doctor.
   Advanced Ss can write specific information they want to know on index cards. Each S randomly draws a card and carries out the request; e.g., an S may want to find out the bus schedule from Boston to Atlanta.
   Intermediate or advanced Ss write situations on index cards for each other to draw and act out extemporaneously in pairs using the telephone.

Special considerations
   Ss will need to know how to tell time to be able to do this activity.

ACTIVITY 70

What's It For? Level BIA

Investment Ss bring in objects and ascribe imaginative uses to them.

Options
Grammar WH questions, modals, indefinite pronouns.

Materials Various items brought to class, e.g., things found at home or in the classroom.

Procedure
1. Ss and T bring to class simple objects which could have several imaginative uses other than what they were intended for.
2. T puts these objects into a large basket or box, raised or covered so that the Ss cannot see them.
3. Ss sit in a large circle. Each S goes to the basket and removes an object without seeing it in advance.
4. Ss reflect silently on possible uses for their objects. (Practical or normal functions are not allowed.) For example, a record album cover could be used as a hat, tray, or a giant envelope.
5. One S at a time "shows and tells" the class what possible fantasy use his/her item has. When that S has exhausted all his ideas, other Ss may make their suggestions. This process continues until everybody in the circle has had a turn.

Variations
Ss break up into groups of four or five, using their items in an imaginative way in skits they will perform for the rest of the class.

ACTIVITY 71

Fairy Godmother

Investment   Ss take turns role-playing the Fairy Godmother and granting wishes of fellow Ss.

Options
Grammar   Conditionals.

Theme   Dreams and wishes.

Materials   Ruler or wand (optional).

Procedure
1.   T role-plays the Fairy Godmother and asks a S to make a wish. Uses the formula: "I am your Fairy Godmother. What is your wish?"
2.   S replies, making a wish, e.g., "I wish I were . . ."
3.   T then asks the same S why he has this particular wish. S replies using an *if* clause, e.g., "If I were . . . , I would be . . ."
4.   T grants S's wish, and then asks him/her to tell the class what is happening at this moment.
5.   S replies using the present progressive tense, e.g., "I'm . . ."
6.   Other Ss take on the role of the Fairy Godmother and ask similar questions of the Ss.

ACTIVITY 72

Request a Service

Investment Ss make up requests in dealing with professionals.

Options
Grammar Modals, reported speech, WH questions.

Vocabulary Polite forms, titles, functions, professions.

Theme Introductions, manners.

Culture How to request services in different cultures.

Materials 3×5 index cards, each with the name of a profession or job written on it, e.g., doctor, dentist, mechanic, florist.

Procedure
1. T distributes one card to each S, or the Ss may draw from a pile face down on the desk.
2. T explains to the Ss that the professions written on their cards represent new identities and that they should not reveal them to each other. T then collects the cards.
3. T redistributes the same cards to the Ss, making sure that they receive a different one. This second time the Ss are told that the professional on the card is someone that they must contact for a particular service.
4. The Ss assuming the identity on their first cards circulate among the "professionals," ask questions, and try to find the professional on their second cards to request a service, e.g., "I'm looking for a mechanic to fix my car." "Do you know where I can find one?"
5. After Ss have found the professional they need and have made their requests, they sit in a circle, state their assumed identity, and report on the services they were asked to perform.

Variations
Advanced Ss can discuss and compare how to make polite requests in their own countries and in the target language culture.

The lesson could emphasize modals for making requests more polite.

ACTIVITY 73

Cross-Cultural Skits

Level IA

Investment   Ss plan and act out incidents that happened to them and led to cross-cultural misunderstandings.

Options
Culture   Cross-cultural incidents which the Ss have experienced.

Materials   None, or optional simple props.

Procedure
1. Ss divide into small groups, and each S describes a cross-cultural incident that has happened to him/her.
2. Each group selects one of the incidents that happened to someone in that group and plans how it will dramatize it. (The S who was really involved in the incident will not play own part.)
3. Each group performs its skit. The class tries to guess to whom the incident happened.
4. The class then discusses the incident and its cross-cultural implications.

Variations
    Ss can write up cross-cultural incidents that happened to them and put them in a box. A pair or small group of Ss can draw an incident and act it out, with discussion following.

ACTIVITY 74

Extemporaneous Acting

Level IA

Investment   Ss write and perform their own dialogues.

Options
Pronunciation   Stress and intonation

Grammar   Any focus of teacher's choice.

Theme   Ss may decide on a theme before beginning the activity.

Materials   3×5 index cards.

Procedure
1. Ss divide into two groups, A and B.
2. Each group discusses and plans a short dialogue for Ss in pairs from the other group to perform.
3. Each group writes its dialogue on two index cards, so each speaker has a copy. At the bottom of the cards the groups write separate instructions on how each speaker should read his/her part, e.g., happily for speaker 1, sadly for speaker 2.
4. All of Group A is asked to leave the room.
5. Group B then invites two Ss from Group A to return to the classroom. Group B gives each of them a copy of their dialogue to perform.
6. The two Group A Ss then act out Group B's dialogue as best they can, according to the directions for the speaker on each card.
7. The same procedure continues with other Ss in pairs from Group A performing the dialogue.
8. Group B then votes on the best performers in Group A.
9. Group B leaves the class and performs Group A's dialogue following the same procedure.

VIII Miscellaneous

ACTIVITY 75

Spin-a-Question

Investment   Each S spins a question and answers it. T may use this as a language diagnostic tool, or as review.

Options

Grammar	Verb tenses (general).
Vocabulary	Shows T Ss' vocabulary knowledge.
Theme	Any theme, e.g., vacations, jobs.
Culture	This activity can be used to tell the T what contact Ss have had with target language and culture.

Materials   A large round cardboard circle, divided into quadrants with a dial in the middle that spins. Each quadrant contains a question that focuses on the lesson. The questions in this circle focus on the Ss' contact with the target language and culture.

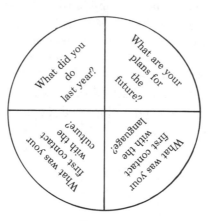

Procedure
1. T has each S in turn spin the dial and answer the question in the quadrant where it stops.
2. While each S is speaking, T discreetly takes notes of areas of S's language weaknesses.

3. After each S has spoken, the T summarizes what the S has said, which can be an indirect form of correction.

4. After all the Ss have spoken once, they can spin again for another question.

Variations

Each question may focus on a different verb tense or specific grammar point.

Ss can make up the questions to be spun.

ACTIVITY 76

Warm-up Exercises
(useful for calming the class)

Investment   Ss may give directions to one another for doing warm-ups.

Options
Grammar   Imperatives, adverbs.
Vocabulary   Parts of the body.

Materials   Records or tapes of classical music (optional).

Procedure
1. At the beginning of class, T models and gives directions to Ss on physical exercise. (Simple breathing and stretching movements are especially good for warm-ups.)
2. When Ss have learned exercises, individual Ss can assume the role of the T.

Variations
    Ss can make up own exercises to lead the class.
    T plays classical music while doing exercises. This has a very soothing effect.

ACTIVITY **77**

Idioms to Music

Investment   Ss think of idioms that they will sing to the tune of a familiar song.

Options
Vocabulary   Idioms

Materials   3×5 index cards, tape of song familiar to all of the Ss (optional).

Procedure
1. Ss brainstorm idioms they have encountered in and out of class. T can limit the number if necessary.
2. As the T writes the idioms on the blackboard, a S copies each one onto separate index cards.
3. When Ss have finished brainstorming, they take one idiom at a time and put it in a sentence in its proper context.
4. T then takes the index cards with the idioms and tapes them to the blackboard from left to right.
5. T asks Ss to come up with the names of songs familiar to them in either their own or the target language. After they pick their favorite of these songs, they sing it through.
6. T then tells the Ss they will sing the idioms in the order they are on the blackboard to the tune of this song.
7. T asks for a S volunteer to direct and hum the song, in order to keep the other Ss on the beat and in tune.
8. Ss practice singing the idioms.

Special considerations
Ss should have already been taught and exposed to a number of idioms.

ACTIVITY 78

Paired Interviews
on the First Day of Class

Level IA

Investment Ss interview and introduce one another to their classmates.

Options

Grammar T uses this opportunity to see what grammar and vocabulary the Ss already know, e.g., verb tenses.

Theme Introductions.

Culture This exercise could lead to a discussion about what are appropriate interview questions in varying cultures.

Materials Butcher paper, felt markers.

Procedure

1. T tells Ss to break into pairs to interview each other, e.g., find out names, nationalities, interests, where they are from.

2. Each pair then introduces one another to the class.

Variations

After S pairs have interviewed each other, they then select another pair of Ss and introduce each other reciprocally.

Each pair writes the information about each other on separate pieces of butcher paper, large enough for all class members to see. They may decorate if they wish. Ss then post interview sheets on the wall.

ACTIVITY 79

Who Done It?

Investment   Ss alter the physical arrangement of the classroom so that they can describe it using the passive voice.

Options
Grammar   Passive voice and modal passives.
Vocabulary   Words pertaining to the classroom.

Materials   Classroom objects and furniture, Cuisenaire rods.

Procedure
1.   T sends one or two S volunteers out of the classroom at a time while the remaining Ss change the arrangement of the furniture.
2.   The T then asks the absent Ss to come back into the room, and queries them as to whether anything has changed while they were away.
3.   The S volunteers will most likely reply, "You (or someone) opened the window," etc. At this point T should answer, "I didn't open the window," and asks them pointedly, "Who opened the window?" They will probably answer: "I don't know." T then says, "The window was opened," and writes it on the blackboard.
4.   T asks the S volunteers what other changes they have noticed in the classroom. If they still persist in making the agent their subject, e.g., "Someone put a chair on the desk," the T writes on the blackboard, "The chair _____ _____ _____ _____ _____ ." If the S volunteers cannot come up with the correct passive response, other Ss may help.
5.   After this procedure has been repeated with the other S pairs a few more times, Ss can continue talking about changes in the classroom, or they break up into small groups and do the following exercises: As an S in each group turns his back, the other Ss make a simple rod construction for him to describe using the passive voice.

Variations
T asks Ss to look for examples of the passive in newspapers, ads, textbooks, etc.

Ss can get practice in the use of modal passives in a discussion of such subjects as "City planning in the Ss' own towns or cities of target language culture," e.g., "New hospitals must be built, a telephone service should be put in."

Ss talk about pictures that could stimulate the use of the passive, e.g., an automobile accident.

ACTIVITY 80

Comparison Shopping

Investment   Ss select items they will shop for in the community.

Options

Grammar   Comparatives, quantifiers, count and noncount nouns, WH and yes/no questions.

Vocabulary   Words used for shopping.

Theme   How to get the best buy for the money.

Culture   Ways of getting "good buys" in different societies.

Materials   Newspaper advertisements, advertising flyers.

Procedure
1. Ss discuss with the T the types of shops and stores they know about in the target language community. T lists these on the blackboard.
2. T also lists and describes other types of consumer outlets or shops that Ss may not know, e.g., factory outlets, thrift shops, used car dealers.
3. T asks Ss to break up into pairs to decide on an item to shop for.
4. Ss look over the newspapers that T has provided to see if there are any shops or stores offering bargains for the items they have chosen.
5. The S pairs go into the community to find the best value for the money for their item, taking notes on prices and quality for reporting to the class. Their findings could focus on why certain stores are better than others, which brands appear superior, etc.
6. Ss report their findings to the class.

Variations

Lesson can focus on supermarket shopping, using coupons, comparing brands.

Adult Ss can use the same procedure to "comparison shop" for an apartment to rent.

This exercise can be reinforcement of quantifiers and comparatives. Ss should use these forms in their reports, either written or verbal.

Special considerations

The foreign language class that isn't in a target language community can use ads in target language newspapers. If the foreign language class is in a metropolitan area, they can shop in local ethnic communities.

This activity could be used for a language summer session abroad.

Grammar Index

This index lists the grammatical focuses suggested in each activity.